Y0-BBX-270

My thanks to:

Battle Creek Civic Recreation who gave me my first teaching job and the opportunity to produce a city-wide talent show in 1967. You gave me the chance to begin my dream.

Thanks to *my parents*, Dorothy and Chet Kajcienski, for **EVERY-THING!**

Thanks to *Angel Roberts* for being a princess.

Thanks to *Adam Roberts* for being a prince.

Thanks to the truly special people who I not only work with but enjoy and respect, *Lana Behrend, Tad Price, Rob Fleeger, Danny Lipps, Vicki Tharrington, Andrea English, Annette Sigmon, Keith Kim, Cathy Kim, John Kim, Chris Peronto, Carol Hayes, Jack Markham, Mike Durham, Greg Kajcienski, Mike Webb, Lois Brady, Doug Bowman, Chris and Boyd Hayes, Mary Styles, Mike Butts, Debra Moore, Christian O'Briant, Lee Ellis, Caroline Toy, Don and Sherry Adams, and Ed and Nan Bowles.*

Thanks to *Minga and Mac McMillan and Don and Gerry Roberts* for the encouragement of my talent.

Thanks to my broccoli and corn friends who have never let me down.

Thanks to *Martha Pullen* for teaching me in every ordinary day there's a handful of miracles.

Thanks to my special kids, *Tricia Houston, Wendy Hain, Darlene Gilcrest, Cassy Barlow, Mandy Mayer, Linda, Debbie, Julie, Vicki, Brenda McIntyre, and Hiliary Levey.*

Thanks to *Emma Samms* for making our 1989 Showstopper T.V. show so successful.

Thanks to our judges who have given wisdom, love, and encouragement, and have challenged young dancers to set high goals and dream loftier dreams. *You have made a difference . . . Debbie Allen, Saucier Baptiste, Moreen Brown, Debbie Pearce Blummer, Robert Burnett, Susan Cantalupo Dewier, Debra Carlson, Buddy*

1

Casimano, Nora Cherry, Mary Lou Christensen, Cindy Cook, Quisa Davis, Lisa Danias, Diane Duncan, Pam Eldred, Scott Fless, Paul Franklin, Greg Ganakis, Eileen Grace, Alice Grant, Douglas Grant, Madonna Grimes, Christine Grogis, Scott Grossman, Ron Hess, Judine Hawkins, Raymond Harris, Dr. Elizibeth Hetherington, Violet Holmes, Gigi Hunter, Pam Khoury, Elizabeth Kovacks, Elaine Guy, Wayne Lancaster, Dee Dee Lang, La Chanze, Shelly LaCoss, Austin Little, Larry Loeber, JoAnn Keyton, Joseph Kenaan, Kim Kimble, Christy Lane, Dan Mojica, Mark Martinez, Mary McCatty, Don Mueller, Kim Nazarian, Duncan Noble, Patti Nordin, Joanie O'Neil, Jan O'Janpa, Richard Ostlund, Tammy and Rick Pessagno, Chris Peterson, Ellen O'Quinn, Anna Graham Reynolds, C.E. and Elaine Smith, Melisa Stewart, George Ann Simpson, Neil Sheridan, John Salvatore, Roger Preston Smith, Val Taguding, Keith Tyrone, Lisa Marie Todd, Julian Thorn, Jean Whitaker, Jo Wiseman, Debbie Wood, and Terry Yates, Bonnie Walker.

Thanks to *Debbie and Diane Gibson* for supporting Showstopper and teaching me it takes a handful of dreams and a lot of hard work.

Thanks to *Mickey Rooney* for your inspiration.

Thanks to *Susan Epstein and Taffys* for supplying America with the most beautiful dance costumes.

Thanks to *Richard Ostlund and Don Muller* for my big T.V. breaks.

Thanks to *Mikhail Baryshnikov* for teaching me that life is the greatest show on earth, embrace it.

Thanks to the special people who make special things happen: *Vick Tharrington, Lisa Canning, Savion Glover, Yvette Glover, The Yarnells, Amelia Johanson, Lisa Danias, J.P. Parker, Michael Peters, Michael Rooney, and Joanie O'Neil.*

Thanks to *Pam Eldred*, the most beautiful Miss America.

Thanks to *Michele Houck* for her program book help and ideas.

Thanks to my dear friend, *Adrian Rosario*, who is gone but never forgotten.

Thanks to *Dance Teacher Now* Magazine for all your support.

Thanks to the beautiful people in Archdale, North Carolina, who make my studio such a happy place.

Thanks to *Nia Peoples* for teaching me those who reach touch the stars.

Thanks to *Keith Stewart* for being fierce!!!

Thanks to the *Ballet Maker "Capezio" family* for believing in my dream.

Thanks to all the SHOWSTOPPER DANCERS – you are the *best*!

Thanks to all the GREAT DANCE TEACHERS who are the real unsung heroes.

Most of all thanks to *Dave Roberts*, my partner, whose passion, skill, wisdom, and heart both in business and out contributed not only to the writing and thinking of this book, but to Showstopper and its great achievements.

Dear Teachers:

Our future is so important, and our children need unique, special, and enthusiastic people who have the gift to teach. Hang in there, and stay dedicated!

We must support each other; teachers supporting teachers, colleagues supporting colleagues. Stay away from an emphasis on the problems, and go back to an emphasis on teaching.

We are special people, and I think that's important. We're not alone. Our aim is the same – helping children fulfill their dreams. If that aim is for a better world, then we must work together. We must care about each other as teachers.

We give strength, power, and energy to life. We teach children that they have the potential to fulfill their dreams and that they can do great and marvelous things if they use their minds and bodies. We are a big part of children's lives during a very formative stage in their development.

Teaching is a reward in and of itself that nothing can ever replace.

Remember, children will always be worth whatever it takes.

Debbie Roberts

4

Contents

Chapter Four
How to Solve Problems in Your Studio

Chapter Five
Taxes and Insurance

Chapter Six
S meth ng cou d be mis ing
fr m yo r d nce st dio!

Chapter Seven
Whistle While You Work!

Chapter Eight
Failure = Success

Chapter Nine
Positive Teaching

Chapter Ten
Extra Money Ideas

Chapter Eleven
Mind Your Business!

Chapter Twelve
Teacher's Survey

Chapter One
It All Starts With You!

Build a Positive Self-Concept

Positive and Negative Emotions

Effective Leadership

Guilt . . . Get Rid of It

The Company You Keep . . .

Learn from Others

Motivational Tapes

Professional Image

Networking

Body Language

Burnout

Human Relations

Be Gracious

Public Speaking

Be Refined

Sell What You Love

It All Starts with You!

Chapter One
It All Starts With You!

Before you waste your time trying to gain wealth, health, happiness, youth, beauty, or talent, let me tell you the most valuable thing you can ever possess is the self-image of yourself as a winner in life, as a contributor to the betterment of mankind, as an achiever of worthwhile goals, and a teacher to the children of the world. Until you have that image of yourself, nothing worth having will stay with you for long.

Building a Positive Self-Concept

A positive mental attitude is an absolute indispensable prerequisite for success as a dance teacher. Winners make a habit of manufacturing their own positive expectations well in advance of the event. If you make it a habit of always expecting the best out of everything you do, you have *one* of the keys to a successful life. Unless you have confidence in yourself as a teacher, you are forbidding others to have confidence in you. Everyone wants to hire, buy from, depend on, be friends with, invest in, trust, and take dance from people who have confidence in themselves.

Positive and Negative Emotions

Draw upon the positives and avoid the *negatives* when giving instructions to your subconscious mind.

★★ Major Positive Emotions	Major ★★ Negative Emotions (To be avoided)
Energy	Laziness
Desire	Fear
Faith	Jealousy
Love	Hatred
Enthusiasm	Revenge
Romance	Superstition
Hope	Anger
Excitement	Depression

Positive and negative emotions will not occupy the mind at the same time. One or the other must dominate. Form the habit of applying and using the positive emotions. Eventually, they will dominate your mind so completely that the negative cannot enter it.

★ A positive mental attitude is an absolute indispensable prerequisite for success.

★ One's need for meaning and purpose is the greatest single drive in human nature and promotes a feeling of personal fulfillment.

★ The root of all personality problems, all behavioral problems, and all difficulties in interactions with other people is low self-esteem.

★ Carry yourself as though you have self-confidence, enthusiasm, power, and vitality, and within a few minutes you'll actually have the feelings that are consistent with those attributes.

Effective Leadership

The title of "leader" or "studio director" must be earned by inspiring and motivating people to give their best. Effective leaders bring out the best in people by stimulating them to achieve what they thought was impossible. You are a leader of your many students and their families, also teachers and assistant teachers at your studio, and your community.

One of the most powerful motivating tools available to managers and leaders is positive reinforcement.

★★ **Characteristics of:** ★★

A Leader	A Follower
Good listener	Good talker
Accessible	Hard to find
Decisive	Avoids decisions
Gracious	Self promoting
Keeps it simple	Makes it complicated
Optimistic	Pessimistic
Gives credit	Takes credit
Confronts problems	Avoids problems
Speaks directly	Manipulates
Acknowledges mistakes	Blames others
Says "yes"	Explains why it can't be done
Enthusiastic	Placid
Positive attitude	Negative attitude

Guilt . . . Get Rid of It

Many dance teachers feel guilty about not being at home with their families in the evening. You should feel that business ownership offers you a number of advantages that are not so readily available in a more traditional job. When the need arises, you can arrange more flexible hours, schedule more time with kids, bring kids to work, or provide part-time jobs for older sons and daughters.

Look at it this way:

1. Children of entrepreneurs (dance teachers) can visit the work place at any time. Such visits offer a unique opportunity to learn about the business world.

2. Children are encouraged to help at the family business. Such work allows them to develop unusual skills and positive work habits at an early age.

3. Assisting with a family business helps children develop a greater sense of responsibility and independence.

4. Children who visit their mother's business have a greater possibility of understanding her work and the demands made on her life.

5. The business owner can, when necessary, create a somewhat flexible schedule.

6. An entrepreneurial mother offers children an interesting and unusual role model. (Studies show entrepreneurial kids are more successful in life.)

7. Children who help their mother at work develop a sense of sharing in a family endeavor and become better workers themselves.

The Company You Keep . . .

Your personality is like a magnet . . . you attract exactly what you send out.

Do not have friends who drag you down, or people telling you what you can't do, telling you you're not good enough or talented enough.

Stay away from people who don't encourage and support you. Associate with people who are good influences in your life. Have friends who make you feel good, *who make you laugh.*

So many people are suffering from their own sense of failure, they want to drag you down.

Being around positive people will keep you motivated.

Network with positive people; they will inspire you to press on.

Get into the habit of holding only positive conversation, and try to avoid idle gossip. It will only bring you down.

It is vital to your success that you surround yourself with happy, supportive, outgoing, talented people. Keep your batteries charged; associate with enthusiastic individuals.

Learn from Others

Find someone who has the success you want, and study what they do. Well-meaning family and friends will give you advice, but remember – if they have never owned a business or run a studio, their advice is probably worthless.

Imitate successful people; watch how they operate. Pay attention to the way successful people present themselves. Learn from them. Learn from unsuccessful people as well. Find out what they do, and don't do it.

You may be surprised how much people are prepared to help you when they see that you are serious about helping yourself. Knowing how to ask for help aids our ability to receive it.

I view Showstopper as a valuable aid for teachers reaching out to get help from each other. Showstopper is a great meeting place and learning tool for teachers.

An invaluable forum for teacher development is the national teacher seminar held at Showstopper National Finals, bringing together hundreds of dance teachers from around the United States. The format of the seminar encourages teachers to share program books from recitals, photographs of their studio interior, and general ideas about running a business. It presents an opportunity for all studio owners, whether from large or small facilities, to voice their problems and brainstorm about how to improve the industry.

Motivational Tapes

I also advocate listening to motivational tapes whenever convenient. There are dozens of excellent tapes available that will encourage, stimulate, and reinforce your positive attitude.

I listen to tapes daily while traveling or driving my car, which I figure is time that is wasted anyway.

Some of my favorite tapes and other resources are:

Tapes

Tony Robbins – "Personal Power"
Robbins Research International
5796 Martin Road
Irwindale, CA 91707-6299

Brian Tracy – "The Psychology of Achievement"
Nightingale Conant Corporation
7300 North Lehigh Avenue
Chicago, IL 60648
(800)323-5552

**The above two sources are highly recommended. They include a course of six tapes. Cost – approximately $150.00, but the tapes are worth the cost.

Additional Tapes

From Nightingale-Conant Corporation
7300 North Lehigh Avenue
Chicago, IL 60648
(800)323-5552

"Be a Confident Winner"
Dennis Waitley

"The Psychology of Winning"
Dennis Waitley

"Being the Best"
Dennis Waitley

"Living, Loving, Learning"
Leo Buscaglia

"Possibility Thinking"
Dr. Robert Schuller

"Tough Times Never Last but Tough People Do"
Dr. Robert Schuller

"How to be an Extraordinary Person in an Ordinary World"
Dr. Robert Schuller

"Success and the Self-Image"
Zig Ziglar

"Inner Management"
Ken Blanchard and Jennifer James

Other excellent tapes can be purchased at your local Walden Bookstore.

Professional Image

Both you and your staff must present a professional image when dealing with people. Your competence and expertise are at the forefront of your business. But, as owner, the way you look also counts. You are the major spokesperson for your studio, and you will form the first impression that many potential students will have of your studio. Always keep in mind the image you want your studio to project, and project that image.

Networking

Networking is a wonderful way to develop and maintain friendships. It is also a way to learn the latest in your field. When you talk to other professionals, you discover new ideas, as well as test your own. Often, you will work out problem areas simply by talking to someone else. A new person can have a totally different insight into matters, insight which may not have occurred to you because you are so involved with and close to the studio. Having peers you can call on for support and guidance is an important step in learning.

Networkers can provide contacts, referrals, and sources of information you might find extremely difficult to discover on your own. People are more willing to open up to someone who is a "friend of a friend." In networking, you will find you have a certain core group from which you start, but whose circle will grow as you begin to develop it. Since everything you do and experience is learning, you will soon discover the areas in which to concentrate, and the individual who provides the greatest payoffs, in terms of leads, knowledge, content, and resources.

Again, teacher seminars, such as the one held at Showstopper (see page 14, "Learn from Others") can be instrumental in helping you develop a solid network of dance and entertainment professionals.

Remember the wonderful movie, Miracle on 34th Street, in which Macy's and Gimbels broke tradition by cooperating rather than competing? Both firms ended up having the greatest Christmas profits ever.
Theodore Levitt, Harvard University

Equally beneficial to networking in the dance world is *Dance Teacher Now* magazine. Not only does this trade publication contain information about dance, it also offers practical tips. You may want to run a classified advertisement for a teacher in the professional marketplace department.

Dance Teacher Now always welcomes your ideas.

Write for subscriptions to: *Dance Teacher Now*
SMW Communications Inc.
P.O. Box 1964
West Sacramento, CA 95691
(Subscriptions – 9 issues for
1 year $24)

Body Language

I use body language a lot. Psychologists link bad posture and sluggish walking to unpleasant attitudes towards oneself. But psychologists also tell us you can actually change your attitude by changing your posture and speed of movement.

Watch, and you will discover that *body action is the result of mind action*. The extremely beaten person just shuffles along.

Be a person who shows super-confidence. Walk 25 percent faster than average. Tell the world, "I've got something important to do, I have kids to teach, and I cannot be bothered with petty things."

When I come out of a class and the lobby is filled, my body language says, "I have a class in ten minutes, and I'm working very hard to teach your child the best I can."

Burnout

This is a difficult topic for me to cover because I can honestly say that in all my years of teaching, I've never experienced what I would term burnout. By dictionary definition, burnout means "worn out by excessive or improper use." From what I can tell, burnout happens when teachers get hung up or overly concerned with things that shouldn't matter – when they're trying too hard to compete with other studios, or spending too much time worrying about past mistakes that can't be changed.

When I'm upset or have found myself in stressful situations at the studio, I force myself to stop and think about what really matters – the kids. Teaching children to dance has to be my primary focus. It's why I got into this business and is the part I love most.

Tips for Coping with Burnout
1. Use only the best fuel for your body.
2. Manage your time.
3. Keep "self-talk" positive.
4. Manage your priorities.
5. Learn to laugh at yourself.
6. Cultivate a close family and friends.
7. See mistakes as learning opportunities.

There is good stress, too, such as creative deadlines, or too much business. These are a part of your working life. Good stress keeps you pumped up; it will make you better.

In general, try not to worry about problems; come up with ways to solve them. Dancers are good at that.

Human Relations

My definition of human relations is how you get along with others. Good human relations is pretty simple.

When you relate poorly to others, you will have a problem-filled life, and success comes hard, if at all. If you relate well to others, success comes much easier.

When you're strong at positive human relations, you gain the cooperation of others, and this cooperation is the shortest distance between you and your goals. When too many people are pulling against you, you cannot be a success.

Actions have consequences. *If you treat people in negative ways, they will act negatively toward you; if you treat people in positive ways, they will act positively toward you.* If that sounds simple, it's because it is.

When you master good human relations habits, they lead to a *triple win*: you make others feel better, you feel better, and your goodwill toward others will come back to you.

Be Gracious

Few things pay greater dividends than the habit of exercising graciousness. Amazingly, even though it's simple to be kind and cordial to others, we live in a very ungracious world. The most successful people I know are also the most gracious. They make it a habit to be gracious, polite, and considerate to *everyone* they meet.

Public Speaking

Communication, both written and spoken, is one of the major ways you will sell your service. Speaking well is another fact of your professional image, regardless of whether you are talking on the telephone, making a presentation one-on-one, or addressing a room full of people. If you feel you need improvement, practice is best, and classes may be available in your area.

Be Refined

Being refined is a matter of having good taste. There's nothing that breeds bad human relations quite as easily and quickly as being rude or vulgar.

Simple, mannerly habits like saying "thank you" and "please" are mentally noted by others, especially by those who themselves display good manners. And the people most likely to add value to your life are those who are refined and who appreciate refinement in others. When it comes to good human relations, refinement is another insurance policy for success.

Sell What You Love

Remember – you are a sales person. You may have the best product in the world, but if you don't get out and sell, it means nothing.

You have to strongly believe in your product. One of the most important things about sales is *"you can't sell anything you would not buy."*

I think that's why so many actresses, actors, and dancers fail. They may be good at what they do, but they don't know how to go out and sell themselves.

When kids come to register at my studio, I'm genuinely excited that they will have the chance to learn dance at the Dance Shop.

I know they will love it because we are so great at what we do. I truly believe in what I'm doing.

I think conviction and a passion for what you are doing are really crucial for anyone in the dance business.

It All Starts with You!

Success means doing the best we can with what we have. Success is in the doing, not the getting; in the trying, not the triumph. Success is a personal standard – reaching for the highest that is in us – becoming all that we can be. If we do our best, we are a success.

The upward reach comes from working carefully and well. Good work done little by little becomes great work. *The house of success is built brick by brick.*

★★ Top 11 Secrets to Success ★★

1. Make those around you feel important.

2. Stress your attributes, not your drawbacks; be an optimist, not a pessimist.

3. Never, ever stop trying to improve.

4. Make your enthusiasm contagious.

5. Smile.

6. Motivate through kindness, not force.

7. Forgive yourself and move on; everyone makes mistakes.

8. Never break promises.

9. Be consistent in your policies.

10. Don't let yourself be intimidated; people are people.

11. Be excellent at what you do. Develop a program of which you are proud.

★*"Do not follow where the path may lead. Go instead where there is no path and leave a trail."*

Unknown

★*"If you look for the positive things in life, you'll find them."*

Unknown

★*The greatest satisfaction in leadership – the feeling of accomplishment that means the most when you look back after 20 years – is the satisfaction of building people.*

★*"A true leader always keeps an element of surprise up his sleeve, which others cannot grasp but which keeps his public excited and breathless."*

Charles de Gaulle

★*"Great leaders are never satisfied with current levels of performance. They are restlessly driven by possibilities and potential achievements."*

Donna Harrison

★*"Here is a simple but powerful rule; always give people more than they expect to get."*

Nelson Boswell

★*"People forget how fast you did a job – but they remember how well you did it."*

Howard W. Newton

★"The growth and development of people is the highest calling of leadership."

Unknown

★"The deepest principle in human nature is the craving to be appreciated."

William James

★"Let your heart soar as high as it will. Refuse to be average."

A.W. Tozer

★"Twelve things to remember– 1. The value of time. 2. The success of perseverance. 3. The pleasure of working. 4. The dignity of simplicity. 5. The worth of character. 6. The power of kindness. 7. The influence of example. 8. The obligation of duty. 9. The wisdom of economy. 10. The virtue of patience. 11. The improvement of talent. 12. The joy of origination.

Marshall Field

Chapter Two
Goals and Goal Achieving

Goals and Goal Achieving

Checklist Prior to Setting Your Major Goals

Time Management Tips

Chapter Two
Goals and Goal Achieving

Goals and Goal Achieving

If you become a goal setter and write, think, and talk about your goals on an ongoing basis, your level of performance and achievement improves dramatically.

When you set goals, you develop direction, you develop focused and channeled energy, and you accomplish more in a short time then you could accomplish in years.

Checklist Prior To Setting
★★ Your Major Goals ★★

Step 1: Determine your goal in life, and then picture it in your mind so intensely that it becomes a part of your subconscious mind.

Step 2: Get all the information you can about your goal, the requirements for it, and the possible compensation in happiness, contentment, and economic security.

Step 3: Set the order of things you must do to accomplish your goal.

Step 4: Set a definite time for the accomplishment of your goal.

Step 5: Take immediate action to put these plans into effect. Do it today.

Step 6: Be persistent in your plans. Don't let obstacles stand in your way.

Step 7: Concentrate on a single step at a time to achieve your goal. You must walk before you can run.

Step 8: Check yourself at intervals to see whether you are on the way, and adjust your plans as required by any circumstances over which you have no control.

Step 9: Put this whole plan on paper, and make planning a habit!

Now – make your plan – TODAY!

To help you get organized and on the right track, each night before you go to bed (you will sleep better), make a list of the most important things to do the next day. Then, STICK TO THAT LIST!

When you have achievable goals, every day becomes an exciting contest with yourself. You get up in the morning with a plan for making that day contribute the most that it possibly can to getting what you want from life.

Look at it this way: How is a building built? What has to be approved before one brick is laid? *The plans. Blueprints.* And what, in essence, are the blueprints? They are decisions about what's going to be. Many thousands of dollars are spent making those decisions and getting them down on paper before anyone works on the building. Every life is worth more than any building, yet the average life has no blueprint. No plans. It's just a series of random happenings. Every day is another play-it-by-ear day.

Without knowing what your goals are, you will never know whether you have reached them. Without reaching your goals, you cannot be happy; you can never win.

Developing a successful plan for effectiveness begins with goal setting. It is true that goals and the sense of purpose that accompanies them are necessary for survival.

High incidences of poor health and death are reported shortly after retirement age. After years in a job or career, it is understandable that someone feels striped of his sense of direction and value when retirement is thrust upon him. Many people reach retirement totally unprepared, with no other goals to pursue, and as a result, they rust out rather than wear out.

Contrast the retirement syndrome to the fact that many creative people enjoy much greater longevity. We (dancers) live well into our eighties and nineties, and our final years are often the most productive. Am I saying that we live longer because we are more creative? Not really, but we have an unending sense of purpose and direction. To us, there is always another dance to set to music.

Few people ever undertake the task of setting definite goals for their lives. Setting goals greatly increases the odds of working less and accomplishing more. You must decide what you want, or you are not very likely to get it. In the meantime, you flounder, working more and accomplishing less by frittering away your time and energy aimlessly.

Remember, success is not sudden; success is an every day thing.

Prepare for the trauma of success. Unless you have new goals and challenges, you will get bored, you will get depressed, and you will start sliding downhill. Always have something you are working on and getting excited about. Your recital is a good example; try to make it better and more exciting each year.

Nothing is worse than stagnation; it is the first step toward death.

Setting a timetable is an important factor in the achievement of any goal. "Work will expand to fill the time allotted for it." For this reason, among others, you have to have a time frame or time limit on your endeavors. Unfortunately, this is one of the steps that most people, consciously or unconsciously, delete from their plan of action. A deadline for action is of the utmost importance. It is the essential activating mechanism.

★★ Time Management Tips ★★

1. Plan your activities DAILY.

2. Do high priority activities FIRST.

3. Learn to delegate effectively.

4. Group similar activities to save time. (For instance, do all your phone calling at one time.)

5. Learn how to handle interruptions efficiently.

6. Learn to say "NO" to non-critical tasks.

7. Eliminate inefficient habits.

8. Mark appointments, meetings, and deadlines on your calendar, and review daily.

9. Learn the difference between "urgent" and "important."

10. File papers immediately. Don't let things pile up.

11. Get as much done by phone as possible. Fax or send a quick note to avoid lengthy phone calls.

12. Use waiting or traveling time to catch up on reading and thinking.

★"The most important thing about goals is having one."
Geoffry F. Abert

★"There is one quality which one must possess to win, and that is definiteness of purpose, the knowledge of what one wants, and the burning desire to possess it."
Napoleon Hill

★"The purpose of goals is to focus our attention. The mind will not reach toward achievement until it has clear objectives. The magic begins when we set goals. It is then the switch is turned on, the current begins to flow, and the power to accomplish becomes a reality."
Wynn Davis

★"The reason most major goals are not achieved is that we spend our time doing second things first."
Robert J. McKain

★"Most time is wasted, not in hours, but in minutes. A bucket with a small hole in the bottom gets just as empty as a bucket that is deliberately emptied."
Paul J. Meyer

★"A man who dares to waste an hour of life has not discovered the value of life."
Darwin

★"The first and most important step in improving the utilization of your time is planning."
Frederick Harrison

★"Do not waste your high energy hours. Invest them where they yield the highest payoff."
Author unknown

Chapter Three
Advertising, Public Relations, Promotion

Advertising – Newspaper

Public Relations

Promotion

Clip Art for Handouts or Letterheads

Publicity Stunts

Word of Mouth

Chapter Three
Advertising, Public Relations, Promotion

Advertising – Newspaper

Probably the best advertising besides word of mouth is your local newspaper. Here are some ideas that will help you plan better newspaper advertising.

1. Think ahead. Being the first studio to advertise your upcoming registration is best.

2. What works best in print: get your message in the headlines. The headlines should tell the whole story, including the name of the studio. Avoid blind headlines that tell the reader nothing.

3. Offer a benefit in the headlines. Headlines that promise a benefit sell more than those that don't. The *Reader's Digest*, which employs some of the best headline writers in the business, has three guiding principles for headlines:
   a. Present a benefit to the reader.
   b. Make the benefit quickly apparent.
   c. Make the benefit easy to get.

4. Newspaper advertisements are less effective on Fridays and Saturdays when people tend to be busy. They are most effective on Sundays and Wednesdays; statistics show people read the paper more thoroughly on those days.

5. Don't be afraid of long headlines. Research shows that, on the average, long headlines sell more than short ones.

6. Next to the headlines, **an illustration is the most effective way to get a reader's attention,** the kind of illustration that makes readers ask, "How can I get my child enrolled in dance?"

7. Photographs are better than drawings. Research shows that photography increases recall an average of 36 percent over artwork.

8. Use simple layouts. One or two big pictures work better than three or four small pictures. Avoid clutter.

9. Always put a caption under a photograph.

10. The picture caption can be an advertisement by itself.

11. The following pages are ads you may use.

DANCE (dăns) *v* **1:** The art and business of The Dance Shop. **2:** The process of teaching children style, grace, rhythm and coordination (i.e. The Dance Shop.) **3:** The final product of hard work, training, creativity and fun at The Dance Shop.

Begin today!

Tomorrow's Dreams

THE DANCE SHOP
304 Trindale Rd.
Archdale
431-2017   431-1714

This is an example of advertising that you can rework for your own studio, inserting your own photographs.

Another ad that you can rework for your own studio, using your own photographs.

Good example of how effective a picture is in an ad.

Public Relations

Loosely defined, public relations is the process of getting your studio visibility without the benefit of paid ads. Public relations costs you nothing but time and effort. You can do this through a feature story in the local paper, an interview on a T.V. talk show, a guest spot on a radio show, and by passing out brochures to prospective customers. Don't miss a trick. You must keep your studio in the spotlight.

If you have contacts in the media, use them and keep them. Newspaper stories are very important as they add to your credibility. Remember – the more information you give the news, the better chance you have to get a story. As a matter of fact, you'll increase your chances of a story if you write it yourself. Remember, good pictures that tell the story are very important.

Always follow up with a thank-you note, flowers, dance studio t-shirt – something nice. Keep your news contact strong. You must stay in the news. You can't give up; don't get upset if someone doesn't print your story. Persistence is the key!

One of your best advertising tools is your dancers winning at Showstopper. Send your local newspaper a press release like this.

★★ Press Release ★★

_____ Studio participated in
the Showstopper American Dance Championships
held in _____ (city), _____ (date).
    Showstopper is the largest dance competition
in the world with 60 events annually and over
100,000 participating dancers. Regionals culmi-
nate with National Finals and a nationwide televi-
sion show.

_____ Studio was awarded
_____ for _____ a
_____ (jazz, tap, ballet, etc.) number and _____ for _____ a
_____ (jazz, tap, ballet, etc.) number.
Participants, _____ (names, if
newspaper will include) received group trophies
and individual ribbons. As a result of their first
and second place ratings, the dancers qualify to
compete in the national finals to be held in
_____ (city), _____ (date).

Promotion

You can promote yourself, your studio, your staff, your classes, or all of the above in many different ways.

1. Explore local possibilities, newspaper shoppers' specials, flyers, radio spots, window displays, billboards, community organizations, and bulletin boards.

2. Evaluate a direct-mail campaign.

3. Sponsor civic or charitable events.

4. Evaluate special seasonal promotions (malls, parades, political rallies, fairs, holiday parties).

5. Teach or lecture at a local college or adult school.

6. Develop a free seminar to introduce your product or service (a one-day mini dance convention).

7. Write articles in local papers, trade magazines, journals.

8. Speak before or have your dancers perform at local chambers of commerce, women's groups, trade associations, basketball and football half-time shows.

9. Develop a brochure and carry them with you to pass out to any potential customers you meet.

10. Contact local newcomers club to promote your studio.

11. Yellow Page advertising is a must! (A picture of a dancer is very eye-catching, and no one does it.)

12. Use business cards.

The first step toward increasing sales is letting people know you exist!

Clip Art For Handouts or Letterheads

Ready-to-use performing arts illustrations are a collection of clever, time-saving illustrations that you may use very inexpensively. If you do not use an advertising agency, this book will help you.

Included are 98 ready-to-use, entertainment-oriented motifs ideal for almost any advertising or publicity purpose. Printed in three sizes to eliminate the need for statting, crisp black-and-white line drawings depict dancers in top hat and tails, in classical and modern ballet costume; singers, orchestras, audiences, stage sets, lights and more, and include spot illustrations, borders, and mortised cuts.

Printed in crisp black and white on repro-quality stock, *Ready-to-Use Performing Arts Illustrations* offers commercial artists and designers a treasury of convenient, inexpensive, and eye-catching designs to enhance advertisements, posters, state-bills, publicity releases, programs, and other graphic media associated with the performing arts.

You may buy this book from your local art store, or you can write to Dover Publications, Inc., 31 East 2nd Street, Mineola, NY 11501. The book is a real bargain at $4.98.

Other helpful books from the same company are *Ready-to-Use Banners, Ready-to-Use Headlines, Ready-to-Use Borders,* and *Ready-to-Use Christmas Designs.*

For color handouts, write:

Idea Art
P.O. Box 291505
Nashville, TN 37229-1505
(800)IDEA-ART (433-2278)

Publicity Stunts

An unusual event or stunt can draw attention to your studio, the more unusual the better. An offbeat visual stunt has a good chance of attracting TV film crews and newspapers. Sometimes a crazy scheme is just what the doctor ordered.

As always, send out a news release in plenty of time for the press to arrange for coverage. Make sure you include the subject of the event, date, time, and location, along with background information about the business for the editor's use in preparing the story.

Be imaginative. Remember, you are competing for press coverage with many other businesses and associations. Timing, as well as thorough planning down to the last detail, is important. If the media covers an event that is poorly organized and doesn't quite come off, they are going to think twice about coming out next time. Again, remember Murphy's Law: what can go wrong will go wrong. Arrange for backup alternatives, including rain dates.

Word of Mouth

Word of mouth is your least costly form of advertising but it takes, by far, the most time and effort. It is the most important source of business, and your most effective means of advertising.

Remember:
- People love to talk, and they will talk about you.
- You must go out of your way to calm the irate parent.
- You must make sure your classes are fun and disciplined.
- Give as many good performances as possible at events that attract a lot of people.
- Be courteous to everyone. Never insult students or parents.
- Always be well prepared with good teaching material.

If you keep in mind these simple adages for running a well-respected business establishment, you should have little or no trouble keeping your customers happy. No matter how much you spend on advertising or getting the word out about your studio, nothing will attract newcomers like a good reputation. Let's face it, people rely on their friends and acquaintances for advice on the best hairdresser, the cheapest grocery store, and the most reputable physician. They will choose a dance studio for their children the same way.

Chapter Four
How to Solve Problems
in Your Studio

Parents

Collecting Money

Making a Profit

Recital Fees and Costumes

Annual Profit or Loss Sheet

Branch Studios

Qualified Teachers and Assistants

Job Description

Teachers' Rules

Survey

Jealousy

Teachers Leaving

Ethics

Why Students Quit

How to Win Customers and Keep Them for Life

Students Leaving

Gossip

Chapter Four
How to Solve Problems
in Your Studio

Parents

Almost 90 percent of the studio owners in this country say the biggest problem in their studio is "parents, parents, parents ...." If this is your problem, first look very carefully at what you are doing, listen to their criticism, and honestly assess their complaints.

People's children are the most precious and most important things in their lives. That is why they are so concerned about the dance training they are receiving. This is great, because otherwise they wouldn't be sending them to your dance studio. Effective communication with parents is part of the job. If someone is difficult, turn the negative energy into positive.

Example:

Mrs. Smith is upset because several of the students in her daughter's class have been moved up to a higher level. One of the girls hasn't even been dancing as long. You feel justified in your decision, as Mrs. Smith's daughter hasn't advanced at the same rate as some of the others and still needs a little work on her coordination. Mrs. Smith, of course, pictures her daughter as the next Prima Ballerina for the New York City Ballet.

How do you handle this situation? You could tell Mrs. Smith point blank that her daughter is simply not as good a dancer as the other girls, and Mrs. Smith would promptly remove her child from your facility, never to return. Or you could turn the situation into a positive one for her child. Explain to her that, just as children develop physically and emotionally at different speeds, so do their dancing skills. Although her daughter has learned so much since her first lesson, you feel that she could continue to improve by staying at this level a little longer. With the other girls moving up, she will become the top dancer in her class, which will give her a tremendous sense of confidence in her abilities.

Sometimes it seems easier to avoid difficult people, but this is never a long-term solution. If you learn to assess the person's behavior and *listen* with genuine interest, it is possible to effectively manage every difficult person. Good leaders never avoid difficult management situations. **Please remember, do not let one person get you down.** Ninety-nine percent of the studio families love you or they would not be there!

1. **Make the effort to be an effective communicator.** More often than not, conflicts are created because the parties involved don't understand each other's true meaning. Clear communication will help prevent unnecessary conflicts.

2. **Replace defensiveness with openness.** The best way to discourage such defensive behavior is to appear or behave in a non-threatening manner. The more you are receptive and open to the opinions and feelings of others, the less inclined they will be to go on the defensive.

3. **Do not encourage parents to stay at your studio during class.** Have a small lobby with little or no seating.

4. **Present necessary criticism in a spirit of kindness, helpfulness, and tact.** (Example: if a parent wants a child in a certain class that she is not suited for, you must explain that you are looking out for that child's best interest.)

5. **Mind your own "Dance Business."** Do not gossip about anyone. Stay professional; gossip will only get you in trouble.

6. **Always end a discussion on a positive note.** Express your willingness to help.

7. **Always stick to your rules.** Remember, changing in mid-stream may make one person happy, but hundreds will be upset.
8. No matter what you do or how much you try, there will always be someone who will criticize you. Accept that fact – it is proof of your growth. **The more successful you become, the more likely you will be criticized.**

If you want to work less and accomplish more, keep this simple point in mind. **It's easier to work with people than against them.**

But remember, **not all conflicts are bad or unnecessary.** You can learn from criticism. Don't take it personally, and don't let it destroy you. Many times parents have very valid points, and we must listen and learn.

The art of understanding people can be defined as the ability **to put yourself in the other person's shoes and see things as they see them.** In doing this, you can anticipate the other person's desires and reactions.

This goes a long way toward your success in dealing with other people and in gaining their cooperation and making them feel good about dealing with you.

Successfully resist the temptation to argue and quarrel by:

1. Asking yourself, "Honestly, is this thing really important enough to argue about?"

2. Reminding yourself, **you never gain anything from an argument; you always lose something.** Think big enough to see that quarrels, arguments, feuds, and disputes will never help you get where you want to go.

3. Being a person with high, genuine levels of self-esteem and self-acceptance, naturally and without effort. Then you will obtain the ability to get along with the greatest number of other people.

Make parents feel important. Acceptance is one of the deepest cravings of human nature. If you have a problem with parents, make them feel important and accepted. Win them over to your side.

On the other hand, there is usually a reason for complaints. After talking to thousands of parents, I found their biggest complaint was studio owners not being organized. I believe the key to having few complaints is organization and professionalism. On the day of registration, I have an information and policies sheet that parents must sign. It spells out all rules, payments, dates, and recital – everything they need to know. This is the key. When someone signs something, they *will* read it. Keep a copy, and give them a copy. If there is a problem, refer to the copy they signed.

★★ Sample Information Sheet ★★

THE DANCE SHOP
340 Trindale Road
Archdale, NC 27263
431-1714
Studio Information & Policies 1991-92

PLEASE SIGN AND RETURN

Student's Name _____ Parents Signature _____

PRACTICE WEAR
Practice wear is required for all classes.
☐ Leotard and tights
☐ Pink ballet shoes if you take ballet.
☐ Black tap shoes if you take tap. Tan tap shoes if you wear heels.
☐ White acrobatic shoes for acro and jazz.
☐ All students hair must be tied back and secured for class.
☐ Shoes and practice wear can be obtained at "Tot-a-lot."

REGISTRATION FEE
A $10.00 fee is required with the registration form to reserve class space. A registration is not considered complete and class space is not reserved until this fee is paid.

INSURANCE
The Dance Shop does not carry medical insurance for its students. It is *required* that all dance students be covered by their own family insurance policies and if injury occurs it is understood that the student's own policy is your *only* source of reimbursement.

SNOW OR BAD WEATHER
The studio will not necessarily close for snow days, regardless if area schools are closed, since many times roads are clear and safe by 2:30 p.m. *If in doubt, call the studio for a recording on whether class will be held or not.*

49

HOLIDAYS

Holidays will generally follow school schedules. Holiday dates will be posted and notes will be given to your children prior to holiday periods. **We do not close for teachers' workdays.**

ATTENDANCE

Attendance is taken at each class and recognition is given at recital for perfect attendance. Classes cannot be "made-up" for this award; you must attend all of your regularly scheduled classes to receive this award. **Good attendance is imperative,** as absences and tardiness can hold back an entire class, and the studio cannot jeopardize its responsibilities to the rest of the class for one student. Please make **every** effort to have your child at **every** class. Awards are also given at dance recital for dance participation at our studio for three years and up.

PRIVATE LESSONS

Private lessons are available at an extra charge of $12.00 per half hour or $22.00 per hour to learn a routine for a competition or pageant, for extra technique help, or extra help if classes have been missed, etc. Most routines take at least five or six lessons to learn. *Limited enrollment.*

CLASS OBSERVATION

Parents' observation days will be the first week in December and the first week in May. Observing the class at other times is not allowed.

RECITAL

Our recital will be on May 28, 29 and 30, 1992. Please reserve all these dates now because your child could perform on any of these days.

COSTUME AND RECITAL FEE

A monthly payment of $7.00 per costume and $1.00 for recital fee is added to monthly tuition fees.

Example	1 hour class	$31.00
	costume fee	7.00
	recital fee	1.00
	total per month	$39.00

VIDEO TAPING DURING RECITAL

Video taping during our year end recital is not allowed. The recital will be taped using professional equipment, and copies will be available at a reasonable price. Still pictures are allowed; however, no "flash" pictures during performances.

RECITAL PROGRAM

We are planning another fabulous booklet this year, and all personal ads are due the first week in March. Information with prices will be sent out in early spring.

OTHER

*Tuition remains the same whether it is a long (5-week) or short (3-week) month and regardless of absences. It is payable monthly in advance, due at the first lesson of each month. No statements will be sent out unless you are overdue.
*No gum chewing in class.
*Students are not allowed to go to "Kwik-Way" or other stores in the vicinity, for your child's safety.
*If you have any questions or comments, please feel free to discuss it with us whenever it does not interfere with a class. We are always interested in improving our dance education programs.

Remember, Parents:
1. are a very important part of your business.
2. are not dependent on you. You are dependent on them.
3. are not interruptions of your work. They are the purpose for it.
4. are not outsiders, but are essential to your business.
5. are not a cold statistic. They are flesh-and-blood, human beings with feelings and emotions like your own.
6. deserve the most courteous and attentive treatment you can give them.
7. are the life blood of your business.

When dealing with parents, study these words and use them often; they are the most persuasive words in the English language.

1. **Easy** – Many people are basically lazy and will look for a quick, uncomplicated answer. Example: "I have an easy payment plan for recital costumes."

2. **Money** – People react positively to saving money. Example: "We offer a discount for you if you pay by the first of each month. You'll be saving money."

3. **Save** – Even the wealthiest people want to save money and, most of all, time. Example: "Our new plan of adding costume payment into your monthly payment will save you both money and time."

4. **Health** – Self-preservation is a great motivator. We gravitate toward anything that will improve our children's health. Example: "Dancing is so good for your child's health. It is great exercise and a lot of fun."

5. **New** – Having something new, knowing something new. Example: "We have a new exciting dance program this year."

6. **Proven** – Another no-risk word. Proven assures that something has already been tested and given the go-ahead. Example: "Our recital has proven to be a great learning experience."

7. **Results** – This is the bottom line – where you tell parents about what they will get and what will happen. Example: "The results I'm getting from your child are amazing."

8. **Safety** – Everyone wants to know about their child's safety. Example: "The safety of your child is my main concern."

9. **Learning** – Every parent wants to know their child is learning. Example: "Angela is learning so much this year."

10. **Love** – The thing we can't do without, and the one word that evokes all kinds of emotion. Example: "I love little Adam. He is so smart and works so hard."

11. **You or Your** – The most important words. Example: "Your little Angela is so precious. She is learning so much this year."

Collecting Money

Another problem in a studio is collecting money. One good idea came from a very successful studio in Florida. This studio has turned a negative into a positive. Instead of charging a late fee, they give a discount to anyone who pays at the first lesson of the month. Therefore, set your fee for the month, then offer an incentive for early payment.

Indicate that they will save money (two persuasive words) by getting a discount if the fee is paid by the first lesson. Otherwise, the rate would be higher, after a specified date. Basically, if you're doing a good job and giving your customers a good value for their money, you will not have a collection problem. But it is inevitable that you are going to have a few problems. Your collection procedure should be deliberately planned so that it will move in a regular and orderly way through a series of steps, the collection effort gradually becoming more and more insistent. The procedure should be organized into the following five logical steps:

1. Reminding the customer.
2. Reminding the customer.
3. Requesting response.
4. Insisting on payment.
5. Final action.

Reminding the customer: The tone of the first reminder should be mild, because the only reasonable assumption you can make at this point is that the matter was overlooked. A good method for giving the past-due customer a reminder is a photocopied statement of the account card. This is impersonal and should indicate that the customer is not being singled out for discriminatory action, but is receiving the same treatment accorded all others. (This should be done twice.)

Requesting response: Customers who do not react to the first reminder should be automatically subjected to the second step of collection follow-up after a few days. This message should not only remind the customer of their debt, but also should ask for a response. The tone should be courteous, but the purpose of the second step is to find out why the customer is slow in paying and what can be done to remedy the difficulty.

Insist on payment: As you prepare to take the fourth step, it is reasonable for you to begin to suspect that the customer may prove to be unwilling, and perhaps does not intend to pay his bill at all. You are therefore now justified in bearing down and applying increasing pressure.

Final action: The last step would be temporary suspension of the child or not letting the child perform in recital. This will most likely do it.

Making a Profit

Another big problem in many studios is making a profit. The fees do not offset the expenses and make money for the studio owner.

When you organize your studio and set your goals, financial planning should be of utmost importance. How many students do you need to pay expenses and make a profit? A very simple example would be:

Avg. Monthly Expense   Avg. Monthly Fees/Student
$2500 $20.00

With 100 students, you will lose money and make no profit.

Avg. Monthly Expense   Avg. Monthly Fees/Student
$2500 $30.00

With 200 students, your profit – $3500 per month.

By increasing your monthly tuition and enrollment, you will make a good profit.

Recital Fees and Costumes

Collecting for costumes is another problem for studio owners. My suggestion for a solution that has worked great at my studio is to add a monthly additional charge to the regular fee. My additional charge is $7.00 per month. Everyone pays a monthly fee which includes classes, recital fee, and costume fee. This eliminates any extra hassle at the end of the year to collect money. Most students only have one costume each with a few exceptions for advanced students.

Sample:

Classes	$31.00
Costume	$7.00
Recital Fee	$1.00
Total	$39.00 per month

Realization! You must be a financial planner and have a goal of how many students you will need to meet expenses and make a profit, keeping in mind the correct fee to charge. Through my 1990 national survey, the average fee charged for a one hour class is $30 a month. Plan how many students you will need to make a profit.

Dance Studio
<u>Annual Profit or Loss Sheet</u>

<u>Income</u>

Tuition	$	_____
Recital Fees		_____
Costume Fees		_____
Recital Ads		_____
Dancewear Sales		_____
Other		_____
Total Income		_____

<u>Expenses</u>

Rent	$	_____
Utilities		_____
Insurance		_____
Dance Program Liability		_____
Health Insurance for Employees		_____
Workman's Comp. Insurance		_____
Building or Renter's Fire Ins.		_____
Advertising		_____
Merchandise Purchased for Resale		_____
ASCAP and BMI Fees		_____
Taxes		
Property/Land Taxes		_____
Social Security Taxes (your company's share of your employee's taxes)		_____
Unemployment Taxes		_____
Telephone (including Yellow Pages advertising)		_____
Repairs		_____
Business or Privilege Licenses		_____
Travel/Room and Board		_____
Professional Association Dues		_____
Bank Service Charges		_____
Office Supplies		_____
Professional Services (legal, tax preparation, accountants)		_____
Postage		_____

Donations _____

Cleaning and Maintenance Supplies _____

Interest on Business Loans _____

Records, Audio Tapes and CD's _____

Sales Taxes on Goods Sold _____

Entertainment (studio parties, etc.) _____

Recital

    Costumes _____

    Theater Rental _____

    Program Books _____

    Flowers/Balloons _____

    Ushers _____

    Props and Prop Construction _____

    Stage Crew _____

Auto Expenses _____

Education _____

Payroll

    Dance Teachers _____

    Assistants _____

    Office/Bookkeeping _____

    Other Employees _____

Equipment Purchases

    (You must take the cost of equipment
    and divide it by the expected life of
    the equipment, and deduct that
    amount each year of its life.) _____

Total Expenses $ _____

PROFIT OR LOSS

    Total Income $ _____

less   Total Expenses $ _____

Gross Profit Before Taxes $ _____

It is best to do this at least *twice* a year. First, estimate it before your year starts (call it your "plan" or "budget") and after your year is over.

Many of these items are discussed in more detail in my chapter on "Taxes and Insurance."

Branch Studios

After reading over the surveys I've conducted at various competitions and listening to feedback from several studio owners, I've come to the conclusion that in most cases all efforts should be concentrated on making one studio successful.

Running branch studios is not impossible, but it is very difficult. Having two small studios means double rent, double bills, and double headaches. Remember, your personality and personal attention as a studio owner is a major reason for its success. Spreading yourself between several locations can hurt more than help. Increasing the number of students at one studio can be much more beneficial for the effort.

Qualified Teachers and Assistants

Do not hire too many teachers. Lots of teachers mean more people to manage, organize, and communicate with. Also, if they are only working a few hours a week, the job may become less important to them since they will have to supplement their income in other ways. This can mean less devotion to you and your studio. All this can be expensive and frustrating.

Finding qualified teachers and assistants is very difficult. When your studio grows to the point that you need more teachers and assistants, a good source would be to advertise in *Dance Magazine* (33 West 60th Street, New York, NY 10023) and *Dance Teacher Now* Magazine (The Beacon Building, 3020 Beacon Blvd., West Sacramento, CA 95961); also advertise at colleges, universities, and place want ads in the newspaper. Another source would be students who have trained at your studio.

A teacher is a reflection of your studio and policies. You must conduct a teacher-training program for any teacher you may hire. This is very important. To be thorough, it should last several hours. They know how to dance, and hopefully teach, but they have to understand *your* feelings, ideas, and policies.

For teachers or assistants to do their job well and be committed to superior performance, they need to know:

1. Exactly what is expected of them; a clear definition of their specific assigned duties and the activities for which they will be held responsible and accountable.
2. Where their jobs fit into the total picture and why they are important.
3. How their jobs affect everyone in the organization (example: if you are to call in sick, who will teach your class?).
4. The specific factors and criteria on which their performance will be judged, behavior as well as technical job content. For example, if a teacher has 150 students and 29 drop out, if you charge $30 per month, this means $5,400 is lost over nine months.
5. You must decide what teacher and assistant responsibilities are.

Job Description

★★ Class Instructors ★★

Duties: **To teach class**

1. Prepare lesson plans for each class in advance and follow them. (Use progression sheets for acrobatics.)

2. Adjust methods to students' levels.

3. Maintain class discipline.

4. Provide fun approach to class.

5. Maintain children's safety. (Check equipment and report any problems to director immediately.)

6. Advise program director on possible advancement of students.

7. Praise each small advancement (positive reinforcement).

8. Greet parents and students cheerfully before and after class.

9. Attend staff meetings when called.

Teachers' Rules

★★ What Makes a Super Instructor ★★

To present yourself as a mature, responsible instructor . . . a professional. To act like someone special, because you are!!!

1. Personal conduct
   a. No sitting or lying down while class is in session.
   b. No food or drink in front of students.
   c. Proper dance attire, hair neat, make-up neat.
   d. Enthusiastic positive attitude towards students, staff, and parents.
2. Be ready 10-15 minutes before class.
3. Quickly learn students' names. (This makes them feel special and important.)
4. Never leave a class unattended.
5. Never start class late or let a class out early. Use *every* minute for professional instruction – that's what they are paying for. Always give each student and parent more than their money's worth.
6. Do not answer the phone during class.
7. Do not allow boyfriends, husbands, or children to stop by or sit in on your classes. This is very distracting and does not present a professional image.
8. Have all recital routines, music, and costumes approved by studio director.
9. Always let your behavior and disposition be a shining example to your students of how you want them to act. Never forget you are a very important and influential person in their lives.
10. Don't smoke.

Survey

To keep customers for life, ask the golden question, "How are we doing?" "How can we do better?" Take a survey in your studio.

★★ Survey ★★

Our studio wants to create a happy and learning dance environment for your child. Your suggestions and comments are very important to us.

Suggestions _____

_____

Ideas _____

_____

Improvements _____

_____

Comments _____

_____

Thank you so much for your time and cooperation! You do not need to sign this. Just drop it into the suggestion box on the desk in the lobby.

Here are the most common complaints about dance schools from parents:

1. Teacher is unorganized; parents are not informed.

2. Facilities are unclean.

3. Instructor is rude, hostile, or abrupt.

4. Studio is not run like a business.

5. There are no performance, competition, or convention outlets for the students.

6. Teachers talk on the phone too much.

7. Classes start late and end early.

8. Teachers are too young and inexperienced.

9. Teachers yell needlessly.

10. Bad, or sexy, choreography.

11. Students do not know recital routines.

12. Teachers are tired and lazy and do not demonstrate dance technique and routines.

13. Teachers are smoking.

Jealousy

If I can teach studio owners only one thing from this book, I hope it's that jealousy is one of our most detrimental emotions. If you conquer any bad habit, achieve any goal in the next year, let it be riding yourself of jealous feelings.

Let's face it, we all have a tendency to covet other's gains. Jealousy is an extremely powerful emotion that stems from our feeling entitled to something someone else has attained. When these feelings have some justification, for instance, if another studio in the same town earned more awards at a competition than your studio, they can be hard to overcome. Everyone wants to be the best at what he or she does. But instead of bad-mouthing the other studio or trying to convince yourself and others that the judging was unfair, be openly happy for your competition. Focus all that energy toward making your studio better, not trying to belittle the other studio.

Anyone who clings to jealousy can destroy themselves. Jealousy generates many bad feelings. It is a product of our personal insecurity and low self-esteem.

When we have conquered jealousy, we will be a better and stronger person.

Jealousy is a natural and normal emotion. Everyone feels jealous at one time or another. The essential decision is whether you will allow jealousy to destroy you or become challenged and grow in self-respect and self-worth.

Teachers Leaving

I have found that much of the jealousy in this industry results from dance teachers leaving their places of employment to start their own studios. Friends instantly become dire enemies. This is totally unnecessary and can be so easily prevented. First of all, as a studio owner, you should have enough confidence in yourself that you will be able to find another qualified teacher. Second, you should feel proud that you trained someone who is now able to venture out and start her own business; that in itself is a major accomplishment. Pat yourself on the back.

Teachers also have a responsibility to their former employers no matter what the circumstances for their leaving. Make it clear from the very beginning that you don't intend to be just a dance teacher forever. Let your employer know that five or 10 years down the road, you hope to start your own business. Don't spring your news of leaving on someone with a few weeks notice and expect them to be happy about it. Also, be fair to the existing studio and to yours. Don't pick a location two blocks away, or even two miles away. Build up your own clientele in uncharted territories, so to speak.

I can't tell you how many calls I get a week from studio owners and parents whose entire grievances are rooted in pure jealousy. Learn to overcome it, and you will become a much happier and successful person.

Ethics

Ethical behavior means conducting yourself and your business in a proper, honest, and moral way. It simply means doing the right thing.

Unethical behavior will haunt you in many ways in your personal and business life.

In the long run, ethical behavior takes less time and pays bigger dividends. **Ethical behavior makes you feel good and proud of what you do.**

Why Students Quit

A survey on "Why Students Quit" found the following:
1. Three percent move away.
2. Eight percent move to other studios.
3. Fourteen percent are dissatisfied with the class.
4. Sixty-eight percent quit because of an attitude of indifference toward students or parents by the studio owner, or by someone who teaches at the studio. A typical dissatisfied customer will tell 10 people at the studio about the problem.

Seven out of 10 complaining customers will come back if you resolve the problem; nine out of 10 will be happy if you resolve the problem on the spot.

The average business spends six times more to attract new customers than it does to keep old ones, yet customer loyalty is, in most cases, worth 10 times the price of a new customer. (I now have children of former students coming to my studio after only 14 years. This is what I mean by loyalty.) A happy personality is a must. It attracts people if it's great, and repels if it is not.

How to Win Customers and Keep Them for Life

1. The secret of winning and keeping customers is treating them well and making them feel special.

2. The greatest customer you'll ever win is you, because *the best salesperson is the true believer*. You must believe in what you are doing.

3. The only things people ever buy are good feelings.

4. Whenever you or your teachers have contact with a customer, you or your teachers are the dance studio to that customer.

5. Some techniques to prevent "drop outs" are:

   a. Be aware of problems, and try to handle them before the child drops out.

   b. Be sure the student is in the class best suited to her.

   c. When one class is missed, this can be a sign. Make sure you let the student know how much she was missed.

   d. If two classes are missed, make a call to the parents.

Students Leaving

If a student does leave your studio to attend another, always let them leave on good terms and wish them well. Be gracious; remember, your kindness and thoughtfulness will always come back to you!

Recently, a teacher relayed a disturbing story to me. She had started her own studio after working at another studio for several years. As far as she knew, she had parted on good terms. One afternoon, the mother of two of her former students came to her studio somewhat upset. She had paid a deposit at the other studio for both of her girls before she had heard about this teacher's leaving. When she asked for the deposit back, explaining that she would prefer her girls continue to take with the same teacher, that studio flatly refused.

This situation brings up a good point. This mother was going to attend the new studio for its teacher whether or not she received her deposit back. Rather than refund the woman's deposit, and wish her well, the studio unnecessarily created some very bad feelings. Chances are, this former client won't recommend anyone attend that facility. The teacher at the new studio, however, won a client for life. Not only did she apologize to the mother for not letting her know she had planned to open her own studio, she also waived her deposit for the first year to make up for the money that was lost at the other studio.

Gossip

Another studio problem can be gossip, by or between students, teachers, and parents *about* students, teachers, and parents. Gossip is always harmful, and the only way to stop it is to not participate in it. I found this poem that seems to say it all:

My name is Gossip, I have no respect for Justice.
I maim without kill, I break hearts and ruin lives.
I am cunning and malicious
and gather strength with age.
The more I am quoted, the more I am believed.
I flourish at every level of society.
My victims are helpless.
They cannot protect themselves against me
because I have no face and no name.
To track me down is impossible.
The harder you try, the more elusive I become.
I am nobody's friend. Once I tarnish a reputation,
it is never quite the same.
I topple governments and wreck marriages.
I ruin careers, cause sleepless nights, heartache
and indigestion. I spawn suspicion and generate
grief.
I make innocent people cry in their pillows.
Even my name hisses. I am called Gossip.
Office gossip. Studio gossip. Party gossip.
I make headlines and headaches.
Before you repeat a story, ask yourself, is it true?
Is it fair?
Is it necessary?
If not – SHUT UP.

Author Unknown

★ *"He who angers you, conquers you."*
Elizabeth Kenny

★ *"Be kind. Remember everyone you meet is fighting a hard battle."*
T.H. Thompson

★ *"Constant kindness can accomplish much. As the sun makes ice melt, kindness causes misunderstanding, mistrust, and hostility to evaporate."*
Albert Schweitzer

★ *"True greatness consists in being great in little things."*
Charles Simmons

★ *"The human spirit needs to accomplish, to achieve, to triumph to be happy."*
Ben Stein

★ *"The day you take complete responsibility for yourself, the day you stop making excuses, that's the day you start to the top."*
O.J. Simpson

Chapter Five
Taxes and Insurance

Taxes and You

The Importance of Bookkeeping

Employer Tax Identification Number

Obtaining Insurance

Insurance

Chapter Five
Taxes and Insurance

Taxes and You

Everyone complains about taxes. Since these taxes are necessary, it pays to understand the tax rules and follow them.

Remember . . . if your net earnings are between $15,000 and $50,000 a year, your tax rate in 1992 is between 30% and 50%.

That means every dollar you save by deductions saves you between 30 and 50 cents. No bank in the world pays that kind of rate. An understanding of tax rules is essential to running your business. You are entitled to standard business deductions, which include:

Advertising – Used in any media – letters, newspapers, radio, etc.

Auto Expense – All auto expenses used in business including traveling in the course of business as well as repairs, tolls, parking expense, etc.

Bank Service Charges – On checking or other accounts.

Travel and Room and Board – Given to employees – such as a week or summer dance competition.

Convention and Competition Expenses – You may deduct travel.

Depreciation – If you own your building, you can deduct a certain amount of its cost each year.

Dues – Paid to professional and business associations.

Donations – To charities.

Education – Tuition fees, books, travel expenses required to maintain or increase your job related education.

Entertainment Expense – Studio parties.

Gifts – Recital gifts, Christmas gifts for students.

Insurance – This would include dance studio liability, health insurance for employees, building or renter's fire insurance, worker's compensation insurance.

Professional Fees – Such as lawyer, tax preparer, accountant, etc.

Interest – If you borrow money to expand your business or buy at a better discount, the full interest paid is deductible.

Equipment – On studio sound systems, mats, ballet bars, etc., office or lobby furniture, and office machines. This has to be amortized (spread out over the life of the equipment).

Rent – On your studio, storage space, auditorium.

Repairs – To your studio, equipment, etc.

Salaries – Wages paid for regular employees as well as fees paid to private contractors such as cleaning crews, special teachers, or stage hands.

Taxes – State or city agencies of any kind, sales tax, property tax, and Social Security taxes for your employees.

Printing – Teaching aids, recital programs, books, handouts.

Telephone – Phone costs, long distance calls, answering service, and telephone directory advertisements.

Utilities – Water, electric, gas, heating, fuel, etc.

Merchandise – Bought for resale use in your studio.

To claim these deductions, you must have proper documentation. Keep careful records and save receipts, cancelled checks, and other documents.

The Importance of Bookkeeping

You must keep proper records. The IRS does not look favorably on haphazard record keeping. Do not take deductions without records to back them up. You may have to pay back taxes with an interest penalty.

Here is a brief rundown of some other taxes of which you must keep track. Always check with your accountant for specifics on your business.

Personal Income Tax – If your business is a "Sole Proprietorship" (not a partnership or corporation), and you don't pay yourself a formal salary, no income tax is withheld from your earnings. You must estimate your tax liability each year and pay it in quarterly installments on Form 1040ES. At the end of the year, you must file an income tax return as an individual and compute your total liability on the profits earned in your business for that year. Your local IRS office will supply the forms and instructions for filing estimated tax returns.

Corporate Income Tax – If your business is organized as a corporation, you will be paid a salary like other employees. Any profit the business makes will accrue to the corporation, not to you personally. At the end of the year, you must file a corporation tax return no later than March 15, unless you operate on a fiscal year schedule.

Sales Tax – Businesses that sell merchandise to end users are required to collect and remit sales taxes to the appropriate state and local agencies. Contact the relevant agencies in your state, county, or city to find out which items are subject to tax and how often you must file sales tax returns.

Employer Tax Identification Number

Every employer must withhold income tax and Social Security tax from each employee's paycheck and remit these amounts to the proper tax collecting agency. Obtain an employer tax number from the federal government using IRS form SS-4. If your state has an income tax, get an ID number from the state.

Obtaining Insurance

In a simple business, your insurance needs will reflect that simplicity. Most companies will offer standard business packages that cover you for property damage and loss, liability, and workmen's compensation. For most of you, one of these policies should meet your needs adequately.

The best bet for health insurance involves finding an insurer who represents many small businesses which together can qualify for low group rates such as Blue Cross/Blue Shield. Definitely beware of little known health insurers who promise a deal that seems too good to be true. It probably is.

Although you certainly need proper insurance coverage, *you don't want to wind up insurance poor* – spending so much for coverage you can't properly run your business or make a decent living. Because of this, shop around not only for the best policies but also for an agent you can trust and with whom you can work.

Insurance

The types of insurance you need to be concerned with are:

1. **Fire Insurance** – This is for the replacement of your building, if you own it, and its contents (your equipment and fixtures) whether you own the building or not.

2. **Liability Insurance** – This type of insurance is for payment of damages if you happen to be sued by anyone for something that occurred at your place of business.

3. **Student Accident Insurance** – You may or may not wish to purchase this for your students. This would pay their medical expenses should an accident occur at your studio or during a studio activity. Most people have health insurance, so you may want to make this an option for which the students would pay extra.

4. **Employee Health Insurance** – Depending on your state, if you employ a certain number of people, you may have to make this available to them. You may also want to pay all or a portion of this for them, and yourself as well.

5. **Workman's Compensation** – In most states, this is required for your employees and covers on-the-job accidents.

The subject of insurance can be a fairly complicated one, so we recommend you contact several knowledgeable, experienced agents and go over a comprehensive program with them, choosing the most reasonable in coverage, service, and price.

Chapter Six
S meth ng cou d be mis ing fr m yo r d nce st dio!

Chapter Six
S meth ng cou d
be mis ing
fr m yo r
d nce st dio!

Your Name

Spike Tip Toes School of Ballet. Would you take dance from this studio? The importance of the name of your studio cannot be overlooked, but surprisingly, it often is. The name that you give to your studio can affect the business' chances of success.

Selecting a name is a very personal and creative activity; you are the one who has to live with the name you choose. It's you that will promote and build it's reputation, and it's your name that will be associated with it. A solid name can help give you a head start. A clever name is a form of free advertising. A trite name could be a hindrance to your success.

Your Studio

Tomorrow when you unlock the door to your studio, before any students or teachers arrive, stand back and take an objective look at your surroundings. Is the furniture falling apart? Do you have year-old magazines scattered on the tables? Are posters taped all over the walls, or do you have pictures framed and neatly hung? Is it organized and clean or cluttered and dusty? Until dance studio owners start to view their facilities as professional places of business, they can't expect to be treated like professionals. If you can afford it, hire an interior decorator. It will be worth it in the long run. If you don't have the money, you don't have to start big. Always remember, though, to be first class no matter how small you start.

Answering Machine

Your phone should always be answered during business hours. It is sometimes not possible for a dance studio to answer from 9 to 5. You will quickly lose credibility if your phone is not answered. I feel the best solution to this problem is an answering machine. Answering machines were once frowned upon. As they have become more common, resistance to them has decreased. Now, many people are annoyed if you do not have an answering machine.

Lobby

Do not make the lobby too comfortable and inviting for parents. This can hurt more than help because parents having too much idle time can cause problems. I think having a lobby to impress customers is important but make it small with little or no seating. Wall decor is very important. It makes a lobby feel complete. If you have a diploma in dance, matte and frame it; it looks very impressive.

I suggest you paint your teaching rooms white. Consider the possibility of painting your lobby a color, or maybe just one wall. I have one wall that is painted ballet pink. It has a lot of personality and a lot of meaning, but it is still professional.

Computers

I read a book, in 1980, called *The Small Computer in Small Business*, which predicted the computer explosion in business. Computers are indeed marvelous, but they do cost a lot of money and take a lot of time to learn.

Whether to use a computer or not is totally up to you, but if you don't own one now and lack familiarity, I would not suggest getting one for a new business. It will probably take you 6-12 months to get a business operating smoothly via computer.

Also, I'm not at all convinced that a computer is the answer for the "Dance Studio Business." If your studio handles less than 500 students, a simple bookkeeping system may be more beneficial.

If you go the computer route, the sky is the limit in software and hardware.

Keep some basic rules in mind:

1. First, decide what you want your computer to do.

2. Find good support. By support, I don't mean just maintenance. Choose both hardware and software manufactured by companies that provide easy access (such as toll-free numbers) to knowledgeable people who can answer your questions, in addition to user-friendly manuals.

3. Putting a computer into a fouled-up business will only foul it up faster.

4. Plan to spend a minimum of about $2,000.

5. Don't expect a computer to cure your shortcomings, and don't become a slave to it. A fancy computer will not make you an instant whiz at business. You must still learn the pencil and paper basics.

If You Don't Go the Computer Route

Everything should be written down and filed in its proper place. As your business grows, it becomes more and more necessary for all participants to have access to vital information. Organization of the constant inflow of information is essential to keeping your business running efficiently.

Following is a sample of a simple, but very effective system. When an account is past due, I just make a copy and send it to them in the mail.

the dance shop
304 Trindale Rd.
High Point, NC 27263

Monthly Tuition	_____	
Recital & Costume Fees	_____	
Total	_____	

Student(s) Name _____ Age(s) _____ Birthdate(s) _____

_____ _____ _____

Students Class Day & Time _____

Parent's Name _____ Phone (w)_____

Address _____ (h) _____

Comments _____

	Charges	Payments	Balance Due
Registration Fee			
Sept			
Oct			
Nov			
Dec			
Jan			
Feb			
March			
April			
May			
June			

Receptionist

My feelings on having a receptionist in your studio are that it is only a good idea if:

1. The receptionist is *not* a parent from your studio.
2. Your studio is large enough to need and support a receptionist.
3. She also has other duties to do during the time she is there, such as bookkeeping, cleaning, or other office work.
4. You must manage a receptionist professionally:
   a. She must have regular hours (never take work home).
   b. She must have an attractive public appearance.
   c. She must not bring children, husband, or relatives to the studio.
   d. She must not use the phone for personal calls.
   e. She must be fully trained on studio policies.

Unless you are very careful about analyzing whether or not you really need this extra expense, and unless you manage a receptionist correctly, this can be a problem.

I have 500 students and do not have a receptionist. I use an answering machine, have a 10-minute break between all classes for questions and a wall mailbox for checks, and am a real stickler on having lots of hand-outs for students so they are always well informed ahead of time.

Mailbox

If you don't have a receptionist available at all times to take payments, a great idea is a wall mailbox. Parents soon learn they are expected to place their checks in the box at the first lesson of each month.

Signs

An attractive professional sign in a prominent, well-lit area is one of the best forms of advertising. A homemade sign is a "turn-off."

Dance Floors

We must be very careful to take care of our legs, feet, and bodies, and especially the young, developing legs of our students, as well as we possibly can. Warm-ups and stretching are essential. Also, recommend shoes with as much resilient padding as possible for the type of dance.

The floor is also of utmost importance for shock absorbency, and "grip." There are several suitable options.

1. **A Purchased "Roll Up" Dance Floor**

   Especially good for grip. Some (from Stage Step) are good for shock absorbency also. Current manufacturers we use are:

   Stage Step
   P.O. Box 328
   Philadelphia, PA 19105
   (800)523-0961
   (215)567-6662

   Harlequin
   3111 W. Burbank Blvd.
   Burbank, CA 91505
   (818)846-8888

   or
   Harlequin
   406 Montchiania Rd.
   Box 300
   Montchanin, DE 19710
   (215)388-0666

2. **Wood Floors**

   Most people believe this is still the best way to go. If you are constructing a floor over wood floor joists, a hardwood floor can normally be put right over the underlayment with good results. If you are building one over concrete, you need to use either resilient "pads" or a very firm resilient underlayment first, then plywood, then hardwood floor.

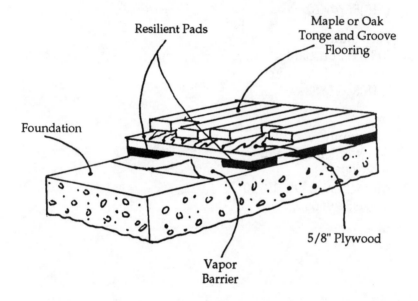

First a vapor barrier, then plywood with 32 "resilient" pads applied to each, then the hardwood floor "resilient pads" can be purchased from:

Sport Floors, Inc.
P.O. Box 1488
Cartersville, GA 30120
(404)387-1543
Resilient pads 2-1/4" x 3"
600 pads/box

Also resilent underlayment carpet padding can be placed under the plywood.

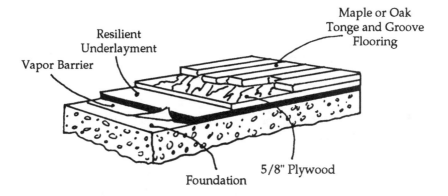

Ownership of Building

Real estate can often be an excellent investment. You can control your building and your future there, and any improvements you make may enhance the value of your investment. There are also tax breaks, such as being able to write off interest and depreciation on your taxes. The best way to analyze your particular situation is to:

1. Keep your eyes open for good possible locations that go up for sale, then;
2. Explore it with both a real estate agent and an accountant.

★★ What Makes ★★ a Super Studio

1. Professional entry and nice professionally painted sign.

2. Always greet people pleasantly, warmly, and friendly.

3. Answer the phone pleasantly. Have the answering machine on when you cannot get to the phone.

4. Tastefully decorated walls; no taped up posters. I'd rather see one matted picture than a wall full of posters (except a Showstopper poster).

5. Sharp, professional, well-trained, enthusiastic staff.

6. Oozes with safety (never leave a class unsupervised).

7. Newsletters, flyers, handouts, etc. . . . very professional, with professional logo.

8. Clean facility . . . especially bathrooms – empty trash can daily. A system needs to be set up so these things are handled each day.

Chapter Seven
Whistle While You Work!

Life is a Competition

Dance Competitions and Recitals

The Do's and Don't's of Dance Competition

Recital Ideas

Chapter Seven
Whistle While You Work!

Life is a Competition

One of the most important things you can teach the students and parents at your studio is the value of competition.

Occasionally a parent will tell me they do not believe in competition. During the conversation, I will ask them how their child is doing in school, and nine times out of 10 they will respond, "She made the honor roll," "She is in the top reading group," or "She is a cheerleader."

Aren't all these activities the result of healthy competition?

It was actually my son's participating in organized soccer that inspired me to start Showstopper. I saw how excited and challenged he was to play each week, how when he would lose, he would leave the game saying, "I'll try harder next week." He learned to practice and work hard to achieve all he knew he was capable of accomplishing.

Failure is an important part of the learning process; it's essential to long-term success. We all compete in various activities on a daily basis, and we all fail. Weightlifters, for example, "fail" purposely as an instrumental part of their training. They lift until they fail, knowing this is the only way to make themselves stronger. Nintendo™-type games are based on losing – you play until you lose and, in doing so, have fun and gain skills. Children don't walk away defeated. They are energized by the challenge and eager to improve. **Without competition, there is little or no progress.**

Dance Competitions and Recitals

Participating in dance competitions, specifically, gives children the opportunity to share their love of dance with other children. I often see children learning new dance steps, sharing costume ideas, or simply having lunch together . . . and loving it.

Competing in local competitions is a sure way to give children the feel of the stage. It's always a little scary to step on stage for the first time, particularly for children. My advice is to take a few "practice runs" before trying to conquer Broadway. This is where Showstopper is helpful. This type of competition gives children a healthy atmosphere to show off their strong points while improving upon their weak points. Performing in front of an audience can also give children confidence they may not have had a chance to develop elsewhere.

Dance competitions create a positive environment. Judges are instructed to give constructive criticism, not to tear apart a performance. Children learn at an early age that whether they receive an honorable mention or a first place, they are winners because they display the courage and confidence it takes to perform on stage.

Recitals and competitions are two of the best teaching tools you have at your disposal. When a performance is scheduled, dancers are much more excited about perfecting their routines. When students have a good reason to work hard, they will. And the best reason you can offer is a performance before friends and family.

Most of your students aren't taking dance with a professional career in mind. They take lessons to perform, and competitions and recitals give them that opportunity. A stage performance is magical for children. Every little girl dreams of a beautiful costume, makeup, lights, and applause.

Parents have entrusted their children to you to teach dance. They expect to see their progress on stage. Younger, shy children especially benefit from public performances; it is a thrilling moment for them, as well as for their parents, to realize this newfound confidence. For the chubby little children who have come to you to lose weight, performing gracefully on stage may be their whole purpose for taking lessons.

A lot of your students would not continue to take a full year of dance if recitals and competitions were not the climax. How many students would quit in March or April? The only thing that keeps many students coming back is the anticipation of performing.

★★ <u>The Do's and Don't's of Dance Competition</u> ★★

The Don't's

1. Don't yell or scream at any dancer.

2. Don't condemn a child for poor performance or continue to bring up past failures.

3. Don't punish a child for mistakes – punishment leads to withdrawal and children often give up dance.

4. Don't expect children to learn immediately – with practice, they will improve.

5. Don't expect children to be pros – let them be children, enjoying themselves and constantly improving.

6. Don't expect children to be immediately courageous – it's natural to be frightened.

7. Don't ridicule or make fun of a child – this only leads to further self-punishment.

8. Don't compare children to their siblings or to more talented dancers on the team.

9. Don't make dance all work and no fun.

★★ The Do's ★★

1. Do be selective about what competitions you attend. Not all dance competitions are created equal. Only attend the best. An unpleasant experience reflects on you.
2. Do make it fun – the more children enjoy dance, the more they'll want to dance.
3. Do be patient – children may initially be frightened of the stage, but with time and experience they will learn.
4. Do make sure children have the experience of performing dance techniques correctly – this develops pride as well as mastery.
5. Do use clear and comprehensive language that the children can understand.
6. Do reduce the fears that children may have by anticipating and lessening their normal anxiety – humor is always effective.
7. Do remember that it is <u>ok</u> for children to make mistakes – it means that they're trying.
8. Do be positive and convince all dancers that they are making a contribution.
9. Do give each child a sense of being special and important.
10. Do provide a role model for children attending competition.
11. Do let them fail without punishment, anger, or showing any disappointment. Support and reinforce what they did well on stage. Failure is a very important part of the learning process.

Tips for Traveling to Showstopper National Talent Competition

Have a planning meeting with parents covering the following:

Cost (competition fees, hotel, food, etc.).
Stress the positive aspect of competition, not winning.
  a. Getting to perform on stage.
  b. Having fun.
  c. Getting to see other dancers perform.
Dates.
Fundraisers.
Chaperones.
Drop-out policy.
Rules for hotel conduct.
All trophies won at competition belong to the studio. Parents may purchase trophies for children.

Have a written travel plan in advance:

Draw up an itinerary for the trip.
Have every detail planned in advance.
Include phone numbers and maps to hotel and competition location.
Designate practice and meeting times.
Issue each child and parent a copy of the itinerary and maps.
Save $$$ by shopping at a grocery store ahead of time. Buy fruit juice, a small cooler, milk, cereal, fruit, and snacks. This will save on eating out.

Recital Ideas

Props

Think twice about building props. Unprofessional props can make a good routine look tacky. I have seen thousands of props used in dance routines across the country. Some have been fabulous, but many have detracted from the number. It can also be time-consuming and costly, and you may find out it was not worth it. So think first.

Preschool props can be simple, clever, and very effective. Sometimes a prop is what preschoolers need to help guide them through a routine.

A good source for recital backdrops to rent or purchase is:

Tobin Lake Studios
7030 Old US 23
Brighton, MI 48116
(313)229-6666

Trophies

Children love trophies. I recommend giving end-of-the-year, participation trophies for students who have been enrolled for three years or longer. This may prevent late year drop-outs. If trophies are out of the question because of financial limitations, you might consider ribbons, medals, or certificates.

Recognition at your end-of-the-year recital can make all the difference in the world to those dancers who don't have the opportunity to participate in organized dance competitions. We call them Achievement Awards.

Tickets

Many studios sell tickets for recitals. It is a great money maker. My survey shows that 68 percent of all studios sell tickets.

However, I feel very sensitive about this because I hear many parents complain about paying all year then paying to see their own child at recital.

Look at the price of your theater. If the theater cost is too high, you may have no choice but to charge. Just be sure you make it clear you're not charging for your own profit, but to cover expenses.

At Your Recital

A polished appearance at recital is absolutely essential to exhibiting a devoted and professional image to your audience, which will most likely be made up of parents. Make an effort to look great. This is the one time of year parents will see you out of leotards; don't blow it. How you look can build up or break down your credibility.

At my recitals, my teachers and I go all out. Any time we step on stage, we are adorned in sequinned gowns. I invite the mayor of our city to present the studio with roses, and strive to make it a major event for all my students. When I'm needed to organize numbers or to help with costumes back stage, I quickly change into regular clothes, but when I'm summoned to the stage, it's back into my glitzy gown.

Above all, make sure everything at the recital is upbeat and positive. Strive to end your year on a positive note.

Chapter Eight
Failure = Success

Winning 101

Chapter Eight
Failure = Success

A winner never labels lack of success as a failure. Successful people are not afraid to fail. They accept their failures as a natural consequence of trying and move forward. **The law of failure is one of the most powerful of all success laws;** you fail only when you don't learn from your failure. Never let failure limit your enthusiasm for trying.

It is crucial that you understand the role failure plays in achievement. If you are unable to risk failure, your chances of success are slim. Most successful people have many more failures than unsuccessful people. But, ultimately, successful people keep on trying long enough to make it. Unsuccessful people give up early and settle for less. They stop daring to pursue their dreams. And thus, the temporary failures become total defeats.

The trouble with losers is that they regard a mistake as such a big event, they never realize failing has a positive side to it. **All great, successful people know this principle about failure. If you learn this, above anything I can tell you, you will be a success.**

History has demonstrated that many notable winners encountered heart-breaking obstacles before they won.

Thomas Edison attempted to invent a filament for the electric light bulb 5,000 times. Did he see that as 5,000 failures? No, he saw it as succeeding and learning 5,000 different things that did not work. So many people give up after one or two failures. They would never even think of trying 5,000 times to succeed.

Behind every successful person is a legend of failure. Believe me, I've had my share of problems and setbacks. I've been disappointed and discouraged. I've run up against obstacles that in no way resembled opportunities. One of my failure-to-succeed stories lasted three years. I had written an article I felt was worthy of publication. After writing *Glamour* magazine letter after letter, totaling dozens of letters, I received one acknowledgment. Persistence paid off. Finally, my story was printed. If I had given up, my copy would still be collecting dust on my desk.

Another story dealing in persistence is my spot on PM Magazine. I had written and written and received only one answer, "No." So I devised another tactic to grab their attention, and my students helped. Just before Valentine's Day, we blew up 200 red balloons with streamers on which I had written "I'd love to be on PM Magazine." I had filled a huge basket decorated in hearts, ribbons, and Showstopper memorabilia and sent it to the producer's desk along with a dozen red roses. At 5:00 A.M., we all went to the lobby of the TV station to surprise and greet the producer. She walked in and asked what was going on. I told her to look on her desk. With the basket and roses were copies of all the letters I had sent with a cover letter explaining my story again. I got my spot on PM Magazine, and they did a wonderful story which later was included in the best stories of the year. Persistence and creativity were the answers to turning failure into success.

Whenever we doubt our own ability to achieve, it is worthwhile pondering the obstacles that others have overcome. Demosthenes, the outstanding Greek orator, suffered from a serious speech impediment. He could scarcely speak. He practiced talking with a mouthful of pebbles, figuring that when he had mastered that, he would be able to speak in public. He became one of the great orators of all time.

Helen Keller refused to allow her blindness and deafness to prevent her from spending her life helping those less fortunate than she.

Abraham Lincoln failed in business at age 31, lost a legislative race at 32, and again failed in business at 34. His sweetheart died when he was 35, he had a nervous breakdown at 36, lost congressional races at age 43, 46, and 48, lost a senatorial race at 55, failed in his efforts to become vice president at age 36, and lost another senatorial contest at 58. At 60 he was elected President of the United States and is now remembered as one of the great leaders in world history.

Beethoven rose above deafness to compose majestic music.

Winston Churchill was a poor student with a speech impediment, who overcame many failures. Not only did he win a Nobel prize at 79, but he became one of the most inspiring speakers of recent times.

The difference between success and failure is most often found in one's attitudes toward discouragements and setbacks.

Use these guidelines to help turn defeat into victory:
1. **Study setbacks.** If you lose, *learn*; it will take you closer to your next goal.
2. **Be your own constructive critic.** Seek out your faults and weaknesses and correct them.
3. **Don't blame luck.** Research each setback. Find out what went wrong. Blaming luck is never constructive.
4. **Blend persistence with experimentation.** Stay with your goal, but don't beat your head against a brick wall. Try new approaches. Experiment.
5. **Remember, there is a good side to every situation.** Find it. See the good side and whip discouragement.
6. **Don't miss smelling the flowers for fear you may get stung by a bee!**

Are You Persistent?

Most people do not fail, they give up. Persistence is probably the single most important attribute a successful person can possess. If you keep trying, you will eventually discover the right way. Calvin Coolidge realized this when he said, "Press on!" Nothing in the world can take the place of persistence. Talent will not; nothing is more common than unsuccessful men with talent. Genius will not; unrewarded genius is almost a proverb. Education will not; the world is full of educated derelicts. Persistence and determination alone are omnipotent. The slogan "Press on!" should be a part of your life.

96

Winning 101

Everyone deserves to feel like a winner – this is about the basics of winning. It is about discovering potentials within yourself, a philosophy that brings out the winner in you. Once you discover you're a winner, you can teach others.

★★ Basics of Winning ★★

Winners have a positive self-concept
Winners have positive emotions
Winners are effective leaders
Winners keep winning company
Winners learn from others
Winners learn from motivational tapes
Winners know how to network
Winners have positive body language
Winners know about good human relations
Winners are gracious
Winners are refined
Winners do what they love
Winning starts in you
Winners set goals
Winners manage time
Winners are not jealous
Winners do not gossip
Winners are competitive
Winners give back
Winners give enthusiasm to everyone
Winners are healthy (diet, exercise)
Winners are fair, honest, friendly

★ *"The difference between greatness and mediocrity is often how an individual views a failure."*

Nelson Boswell

★ *"It is a mistake to suppose that people succeed through success; they much oftener succeed through failures . . . Precept, study, advice, and example could never have taught them so well as a failure has done."*

Samuel Smiles

★ *"I never see failure as failure, but only as the game I must play to win."*

Tom Hopkins

★ *"If you're not big enough to lose, you're not big enough to win."*

Walter Reuther

★ *"Failure is success if we learn from it."*

Malcolm S. Forbes

★ *"True success is overcoming the fear of being unsuccessful."*

Paul Sweeney

★ *"Failure is only the opportunity to more intelligently begin again."*

Henry Ford

★"We learn wisdom from failure much more than from success. We often discover what will do, by finding out what will not do, and probably he who never made a mistake never made a discovery."

Samuel Smiles

★"Would you like me to give a formula for...success? It's quite simple, really. Double your rate of failure... You're thinking of failure as the enemy of success. But it isn't at all...You can be discouraged by failure – or you can learn from it. So go ahead and make mistakes. Make all you can. Because, remember, that's where you'll find success on the far side of failure."

Thomas J. Watson

★"How a man plays the game shows something of his character; how he loses shows all of it."

Unknown

★"They won because they refused to become discouraged by their defeats."

B.C. Forbes

★"What this power is I cannot say, all I know is that it exists and becomes available only when a person is in that state of mind in which they know exactly what they want and is fully determined not to quit until they find it."

Alexander Graham Bell

★"You may be disappointed if you fail, but you are doomed if you don't try."

Beverly Sills

Chapter Nine
Positive Teaching

Building Self-Confidence

Choosing Your Words

Injury Prevention

Preschool Teaching

Music

Chapter Nine
Positive Teaching

Building Self-Confidence

The most important ingredient for teaching is building self-confidence in a student.

I believe in positive instruction and never negative. I have discovered that praising the one best attribute a student may have will cause that one to develop into two, until eventually, the student will feel successful. Screaming at a student will alienate her or him from any desire to dance or perform. Naturally, technique needs to be corrected, but first, point out the positive and then do the correcting. A child is like a fragile flower; if you abuse it, it withers, and if you nurture it, it blooms.

Many times a parent has already deflated a child's self-confidence without even knowing it.

When a child registers at the studio, the parent might say, "Here is Susie. She can hardly do a cartwheel and is very uncoordinated. She really needs dance." This parent loves her child, but does not realize she is telling the child to be uncoordinated and clumsy. Dance teachers should encourage these parents to build confidence and self-esteem at home during practice while they are concentrating on the same thing at the studio. Lack of **encouragement** is the biggest cause of turnover in America – the big reason for kids running away, employees leaving, couples divorcing, and so on.

Encouragement is bringing hope for the future. If you expect the best from your students, more than likely, you will get it. I'm not saying not to be strict. You will always remember the strict teachers. I'm asking you to give encouragement and love.

If Praise Is so Powerful, Why Is There so Little of It?

Chances are, you are criticized far more often than you are praised. It is natural, then, to think criticism is the way to get results. A collection of "don't praise people" myths influence the way we think. Look at them and see how foolish they are.

★ "But the parents at the studio don't praise me. Why should I compliment them?"
   Answer: Because you are a student of success and they obviously aren't. Remember, you need their support. You set the example.

★ "But there is nothing about Sally that is worthy of praise."
   Answer: There is something about everyone that is praiseworthy. Everyone has some good qualities. Find them, and recognize them. No one is perfect, and no one is totally imperfect.

★ "But you can over-praise people."
   Answer: I have asked thousands of people if they have ever gotten psychological indigestion because they receive too much praise. I have not found one. Each of us hungers for more ego food.

★ "But if I praise someone, he or she will put forth less effort."
   Answer: Wrong! Praise a child for a good report card and the child tries even harder. Praise a dancer for a good performance and she will try even harder in the next performance.

You may be a tremendous dancer and a brain when it comes to business, but neither of those things guarantees that you will be a successful teacher. Studio owners tend to have more training in dance technique than in dance education, yet unless you're able to motivate and excite while still making learning your objective, you will have a difficult time keeping classes full.

Compare the differences between a magnetic teacher and a rejected teacher.

Magnetic teachers are inviting. They're genuinely interested in every student who sets foot in their studio. They listen to the children, no matter how young. They're kind yet firm, honest and trusting, dynamic and humorous, yet serious when they need to be. Most of all, they know dance, love dance, and make it their priority to pass that on to each student.

Rejected teachers, as you might have gathered, have totally opposite traits. They're apathetic at best. They're not interested in the students other than to hope they show up and pay on time. They're strict disciplinarians who have little tolerance for children or fun. They teach through criticism and demand results.

Obviously, very few teachers have totally magnetic or totally rejecting personalities, but every teacher needs to analyze how their students view them on a regular basis. There is always room for improvement. You might try an anonymous questionnaire or critique at mid-year.

Five Traits of a Successful Dance Teacher

1. **Knowledgeable** – If you don't know dance, you can't teach dance.
2. **Attentive** – You have to be a good listener. Stop what you're doing and look directly at whoever is talking to you. If you don't have time at that moment, schedule time later. Respond to show you're interested and don't cut the conversation short. Pay attention to how the person is acting – nervous, angry, concerned, etc. – and react appropriately.
3. **Sincere** – Don't say one thing and do another. Don't pretend you're interested in a student's problem, then do nothing about it. The quickest way to turn off students and parents is to be phony.
4. **Understanding** – Do your best to relate to the students. You don't have to be "Dear Abby," but realize it isn't easy being a kid today and show your concern when there appears to be a problem.
5. **Respectful** – Place all your students on the same high level no matter what their backgrounds, abilities, or personalities. Treat each one as if he or she were your only student. You very well may be their only dance teacher.

Choosing Your Words

What you say is often not as important as how you say it. A simple phrase, such as, "Can I help?" as opposed to "What do you want?" can make all the difference in how you appear to others.

Try . . .	Instead of . . .
"Let me see what I can do."	"Give me a break."
"Let's try it together."	"I can't believe you can't do this."
"Can we set up a time to talk?"	"I'm busy right now."
"That's terrific."	"It's about time."
"Because . . ." (valid reason)	"Because I said so."
"That's great. Now let's try . . ."	"Forget it; it won't work."

Injury Prevention

Properly fitting footwear, proper dancing surfaces, proper conditioning, proper medical advice, proper strength and flexibility all contribute to a program of injury prevention. Dr. Carl Stanitski, clinical associate professor of orthopedic surgery at the University of Pittsburgh School of Medicine, suggests that there are six predominant factors that can cause injuries, overuse injuries in particular:

1. **Shoes**: Ill-fitting shoes, etc., which can cause repetitive stress.
2. **Surfaces**: Excessively hard, unpadded dance floors.
3. **Speed** ("too much too soon"): Rushing kids before they're properly conditioned or trained.
4. **Structure** (of the body): Orthopedic mal-alignments, primarily the knees and ankles. Learn each child's body structure so you will know his or her limitations.
5. **Strength**: Inequity between strength and size.
6. **Stretching**: Decrease in flexibility, particularly during rapid adolescent growth spurt.

Preschool Teaching

Dance education for preschoolers has many benefits. It not only exercises the whole body, but also the mind. It not only benefits the muscles, it creates a love for dance that develops into a lifetime desire for being fit.

If you have the insight and energy to get your preschool age children to love learning dance, you've taken the first step in establishing a core of students who will be with you for years to come.

I believe one of the first major mistakes a studio owner can make is to allow student teachers to conduct classes for little ones. You're giving a signal to parents that the preschool age dancers aren't worthy of your time. Children need a mature role model who has a significant dance background, not an inexperienced teenager who is learning the ropes, so to speak, at the studio. I teach a remarkable number of preschoolers at my studio, because I know this is where I can cultivate a love of dance. It's a major responsibility.

Preschool dance hours are filled with fun and laughter, but I never forget that the children are there to learn. My program is a strong one, thus my dropout rate is extremely low. Approximately 200 preschoolers participate each week.

Start with a Few Basics:

1. Don't allow parent observations. Parents can be a big distraction for little ones who are learning to concentrate.
2. Learn to memorize names quickly. Always call children by their names – it makes them feel important.
3. Be flexible and smart enough to know when something isn't working and have the insight to change it.
4. Strive to make each child feel important and special.
5. Break down skills to the minutest parts.
6. Work with empathy when dealing with parents.
7. Be a good listener – even to stories about pets; learn to pick up on fears and adjust to them.
8. Be warm and affectionate – actually love the children in the class through actions and expressions.
9. Be a sharp observer – watch for the safety of the students.
10. Be an ACTOR! Entertain, but keep the group disciplined.
11. Be receptive to training – believe in the program being taught.
12. Be professional in your appearance – make the children proud and give them a nice image to admire.
13. Be authoritative but patient – keep the children in line, but with care and understanding.
14. Maintain a high energy level even on days when you don't feel like it.
15. Be enthusiastic/extroverted – keep class fun!

Keeping their Attention

I've developed my preschool teaching approach keeping in mind that young children's attention spans are extremely short. If children are attentive you can teach; if not, you waste half of your class time trying to keep them quiet. This is why I prepare everything on tape. I have no reason to even walk back and forth to the record player; even a brief pause such as this can break their interest. You must tape all of the music ahead of time, leaving a little space in between each song for instruction. Put the tape in, and go with it.

The kids are always asking, "When will it be time for ballet?" For this, I've come up with a great solution. I let the little ones wear tutus and dance with glittered stars. As "Twinkle, Twinkle Little Star" plays, they put the stars in different positions and parade around the room. As long as they have their tutus and twinkle stars, they don't get bored. All it takes is a little ingenuity to turn a good idea into a great performance parents and kids will love.

What to Teach

My preschool classes run one hour and include a little pre-ballet, acrobatics, and basic rhythm, and movement. I hesitate to recommend starting tap at such a tender age. It involves a lot of coordination and little children tend to get frustrated trying to learn steps before they have learned basic rhythm. Little ones want to be more active than tap allows. In my rhythm teaching, we do little steps including "step up, step back, step side, step together, step, clap, heel step, toe step, etc."

I usually end the class with acrobatics because that is what the children love most. This is my strongest field for preschoolers because it enables them to exert all of their unfocused energy. We, of course, teach the basics – cartwheels, forward rolls, backward rolls, straddle rolls, backbends, etc. – but I found some learning tools about four years ago, which make learning even more fun. On the following page is a diagram of all this equipment.

A basic and versatile tool is the wedge, which is great for teaching front and back rolls and a little more advanced back handsprings. Possibilities for using the wedge are endless.

The beam is great for teaching balance and coordination by having students walk forward, backward, and sideways on it. When the children get a little older and more experienced, I have them do cartwheels and other difficult moves on the beam to enhance grace and balance. It is surprising how many dedicated parents will go home and construct a home-made balance beam on which their children can practice. Other tools I use are the octagon, for which we learn to kick out of back bends at a young age, and the mailbox over which the children hurdle.

We work on these tools each class and during the last 10 minutes set up an obstacle course. Every student is instructed to walk the beam, skip to the wedge, jump in hula hoops placed on the floor, cartwheel out of the hoops, and go on to the octagon. This activity ends the class with lots of enthusiasm and excitement, which makes the children eager to return the next week.

For information on studio equipment and mats, contact:
   Mancino Manufacturing Co.
   4962 Baynton Street
   Philadelphia, PA 19144
   (215)842-0690
   (800)338-6287

Another source for mats only is:
   Van Horneff (V.J.R. Corp.)
   P.O. Box 42
   Waldwick, NJ 07463
   (201)444-3777

Music

  Music is often more effective than anything else in conducting and entertaining a class. When I play certain music, the kids get really enthused.

The dance part of my preschool hour is often conducted to tried and true arrangements such as "Body Rock," "Teddy Bear's Picnic" (using teddy bears for props), "Monster Mash," "Put On a Happy Face" (using happy faces for props), "Toy Soldiers," "The Freeze Dance," "The Sports Dance," and "Animal Action."

Some preschool songs that are hip and a lot of fun come from "Hot Pink Production" that I helped produce. The tape is called "Show and Tell," and the songs are all designed to use props, and are perfect for recital, competition, and classes. Some songs featured and prop ideas are:

Pool side dance

Baby, I'm a Star

ABC Rap

Ready Teddy

Boogie Woogie Man

This tape is a *must*! You can order this tape through:

Showstopper
304 Trindale Road
High Point, NC 27263
(919)431-8017
Visa and Mastercard welcomed
$9.95 plus $2.00 shipping

Other Record Sources

Kimbo Educational
P.O. Box 477
Long Branch, NJ 07740
"My Teddy Bear and Me" (Album)
"Do It Yourself Kids Circus" (Album)

Your local record store or K-Mart
"Minnie & Me"
"Mickey's Rock Around the Mouse"
"Totally Minnie"

The following albums are from Younghearts
Greg & Steve
P.O. Box 27784
2413-1/2 Hyperion Avenue
Los Angelos, CA 90027
1(213)663-3223

"Kids in Motion"
"Animal Action"   "Body Rock"
"The Freeze"   "Animal Action II"

"On The Move"
"Sports Dance"   "On The Move"
(the only songs I use on this album)

"We All Live Together" - Volume 4
"Dance Medley" (the only song I use on this album)

★★ Acrobatic Skills for Preschoolers ★★

Forward Roll
Backward Roll
Log Roll
Knee-Back Bend
Jazz-Back Bend
Backbend
Backbend-Walk
Backbend-Change Legs
Touch Head
Headstand
Split on Right
Split on Left
1/2 Split and Touch Head
Stride
Cartwheel on Right
Cartwheel on Left
One Hand Cartwheel Right
One Hand Cartwheel Left
Round Off Right
Round Off Left
One Hand Round Off
Frontover
Double Front Roll
Front Straddle Roll
Back Straddle Roll
Front Scale
Beam Walk
1/2 Split
Push up into Back Bend
Push up Lift Each Leg
Chest Roll
Dive Roll

★"*Few things in the world are more powerful than a positive push. A smile. A word of optimism and hope. A 'you can do it' when things are tough.*"

Richard M. Devos

★"*A word of encouragement during a failure is worth more than a whole book of praise after a success.*"

Unknown

★"*Appreciative words are the most powerful force for good on earth!*"

George W. Crane

★"*When people are made to feel secure and important and appreciated, it will no longer be necessary for them to whittle down others in order to seem bigger in comparison.*"

Virginia Arcastle

★"*Outstanding leaders go out of the way to boost the self-esteem of their personnel. If people believe in themselves, it's amazing what they can accomplish.*"

Sam Walton

Chapter Ten
Extra Money Ideas

Registration Fee

Parades

Birthday Parties

Retailing

Your Best Money Maker

Fund-Raising Ideas

Recital Program Books

Chapter Ten
Extra Money Ideas

Registration Fee

Most studios charge a registration fee ranging from $10 to $20. This fee is charged to hold a student's spot in the fall classes. It is not deducted from tuition. This is extra income for you. I have found little resistance to this. People feel more obligated to follow through with their dance plans if they have paid a registration fee.

Parades

Parades are one of my favorite ways to generate excitement in the studio. As a dance teacher, you too should love the festivity and magic parades incite. My studio participates in four Christmas parades a year, and as a result, I have very few drop-outs before then. Nearly 90 percent of my students turn out because we make it such a fun event for everyone involved.

Parades can also be a great money maker for your studio. We sell sweatshirts, pom-poms, and hats emblazoned with the studio logo. If you are interested in sweatshirts, a good source is:

A & G Incorporated
2727 West Roscoe Street
Chicago, IL 60618
(800)621-6578

Birthday Parties

Hey Kids!
Have Your Next
Birthday Party At The
DANCE SHOP!!!!

Kids (and parents) have a ball at the Dance Shop!
The 1 1/2 hour Saturday or Sunday parties feature a
professionally trained instructor leading the children in
exercise, dance, gymnastics, and games.
We provide a clean, safe atmosphere for fun activities,
opening presents, and refreshments. For only $4.00 per
child you can treat yourself (and your kids) to a unique
birthday experience that will be long remembered. We will
decorate, give each child a gift, and prepare the birthday
child with a special gift! All you have to do is provide
refreshments! A minimum of 10 children is required.

The Dance Shop
(919) 431-1714

Everyone loves a party. This has been a great idea to bring new students into the studio. It's also a great money maker.

You may take my studio name out of this ad and use your own name.

Retailing

More women head into retailing than into any other kind of business. Maybe it is because they're the number one consumers or maybe it's because they've honed their shopping skills to a fine art. Whatever the reason, merchandising is something women think they know about. When a purchase is made, you jot down the sale, collect the money, and hand over the goods. What could be easier?

A lot of things. The mortality rate of retail businesses is high, and the Small Business Administration computes the failure rate of women-owned specialty shops at 79 percent. Indeed, according to Dun and Bradstreet, 62 percent of all business failure in the United States in 1989 was in the retail trade.

Most stores fail because the owner doesn't know anything about the retailing business. It is a common fallacy to think a clothing shop, for example, would be fun and easy to operate. Successfully merchandising goods is knowing what will sell and how to make it sell in a continuous cycle of buying from one source and selling to another. Competition such as KMart, Walmart, etc., have really inexpensive dancewear. A rise in discount specialty stores selling brand names will also hurt business.

Opening a retail store takes money as well as talent. A good location is essential. If you rent a building outside your studio, you will draw business from other studios. If you open in your studio in a little storage room or corner, you will save on rent, but you will limit yourself to your studio's business. If you have a large studio, this could pay off. Some manufacturers, however, will not sell to you if you open in your studio. They feel you cannot make it, and other studios will not come into your studio to buy. You must have money for inventory investment and may have to go on buying trips. Along with merchandise to sell, you will need store fixtures.

Also remember that dancewear is seasonal. September will be a good month, but after that you may need something else to fill in, perhaps something like children's clothing. It may be a possibility to set up a booth in your lobby for registration and sell dancewear for a limited time. If you buy cautiously, you can make money.

Remember, the major cause of most business failures is management lacking the knowledge, skills, experience, or simply the time needed to run a business efficiently.

I'm not trying to discourage you from opening a retail store, but you must know the facts. It is hard, time consuming, costly, and competitive. You can do it, but you must know what is involved.

For Further Information, Contact:

National Retail Merchants Association, 100 West Thirty-first Street, New York, NY 10001, (212)244-8780. (Their book department publishes a catalog of books, films, and periodicals.) See your library for additional listings for specific retail associations in *The Encyclopedia of Associations* (Gale Research) where more than 25,000 national and international organizations are listed.

Directory of Conventions. Successful Meetings Magazine, 633 Third Avenue, New York, NY 10017. Lists exhibitions all over the country of interest to retail merchants (i.e., gift shows, toy shows, home furnishings, etc.).

Trade Directories of the World. Croner Publications, 211-05 Jamaica Avenue, Queens Village, NY 11428. Lists all industries (gift, toy, apparel, fancy food, etc.) with information on their publications.

Bottom Line in Retailing: The Touche Ross Guide to Retail Management, by Randy L. Allen (Chilton Book Co.).

Independent Retailing, by Harold Shaffer and Herbert Greenwald (Prentice-Hall).

Your Best Money Maker

Through my survey of teachers, I found that 62 percent of dance studios do have fund-raisers. Here are some ideas.

1. Candy sales.
2. Donut sales.
3. Car washes.

Other ideas:

Holiday Catalog Sales	Calendar Sales	Decorate Lollipops
50's Dance	Jacket/T-Shirt Sales	Wrapping Paper
New Years "Lock-In"	Raffle Tickets	Sweetheart Ball
Sub Sales	Parents' Dances	Silent Auction
Dance Revue	Golf Tournament	Dance-A-Thon
Garage Sales	Spaghetti Dinner	Bake Sales
Tupperware	Magazine Sales	Cartwheel-A-Thon
Trash Bag Sales	Cookie Sales	Recital Flowers
Book Ads	Recital Pictures	Jewelry Sales
Concession Booths	Refreshments at Recital	

Fund-Raising Ideas

The most successful fund-raiser has been food, particularly candy bars. Candy bars are easy to sell, and the percentage of profit is usually high.

Wholesale items which are appealing to children can be found in various catalogs. One of the most popular is the Oriental Trading Company. For information, contact:

Oriental Trading Company
Fax (800)327-8904 (credit card orders only)
(402)331-5511
Mail order: P.O. Box 3407, Omaha, NE 68103

Recital Program Books

Your program book is an advertisement, a good public relations tool, and a money maker.

Ideas to help you:
1. Include an impressive photograph of yourself and your teacher, with resume and credentials.
2. Include pictures of senior students.
3. Sell ads to parents to offer their congratulations.
4. Contract professional artwork for the cover of your book.
5. Have your print professionally typeset.
6. Use lots of good pictures of students.
7. If you have group pictures taken, be sure your photographer has a good reputation. I have had a few bad experiences. Also make sure that your photographer gives you a picture of each group at no charge. He will be able to make money from selling pictures. The payback for using your studio should be free pictures to you, or a commission.
8. Charge for the program book – $4.00 to $5.00 is the going rate for about a 75-page book. Parents and students do love this, and it is an easy sale, but start early to promote sales.
9. Look for good printing prices. They can vary a lot. Get several quotes in writing. If you are not careful, you can get badly stung.
10. The *Writer's Digest* may have good ideas for you. It also lists typesetters all over the country that may help you.

> *Writer's Digest*
> 1507 Dana Avenue
> Cincinnati, OH 45207
> (800)234-0963

I highly recommend:

> PagePro Executive Services, Inc.
> Belcher Plaza
> 51 S. Main Avenue, Suite 311
> Clearwater, FL 34625-3934
> (813)461-3450

11. Be sure to check the paper you use; it can vary in price.
12. Printers I recommend are:

Evanston Publishing, Inc.	McNaughton & Gunn
1216 Hinman Avenue	960 Woodland Drive
Evanston, IL 60202	P.O. Box 10
(708)492-1911	Saline, MI 48176
	(313)429-5411
	Sales office: (301)762-7000

Below is sample information to help you sell the program books:

the dance shop

304 Trindale Rd.
High Point, NC 27263
(919) 431-1714

Dear Students:

Again for this year's Recital, we are going to have a
large, elaborate program book! It will contain the
program order, pictures of students, special recogni-
tions, and much more! Last year's book was a great
success, and we are excited to offer this keepsake to
you again this year.

"Keepsake Ad" prices ...	
Eighth Page	$15.00
Fourth Page	$22.00
Half Page	$40.00
Full Page	$80.00
photographs $5.00 additional	

Here's an example of an Ad!

Good Luck on your
5th dance recital,
Jennifer!

Love, Mom & Dad

Chapter Eleven
Mind Your Business!

The Business Plan

The Bookkeeping System

Form and Time-Savers

Pricing

Always Sign Your Own Checks

Establish a Professional Business

Finesse Your Way to Success

Chapter Eleven
Mind Your Business!

The Business Plan

You must have a good business plan to be successful. Before risking valuable time, energy, and money, you need to know exactly what procedures you must use to be a success. Get out your pen and paper, and clearly and concisely analyze yourself, your potential, and your goals. Formalizing your ideas by putting them down on paper will give you a clear picture of where you are going, how you will do it, who will help you, to whom your service is directed, how much you will charge. Although preparing a plan is often time-consuming, you have already done half the work. Now you need to organize your information in a well-written form.

You may already own a studio and have never written a business plan. Perhaps now is the time for you to start. For your studio to grow and prosper, you must establish some system-ized view of its goals, purpose, structure, and budgeting needs.

A. **Your Service**
   1. Why are you unique?
   2. What will you teach, for whom?

B. **Your Market**
   1. The size of your market?
   2. What is the growth potential?
   3. What are special problems and opportunities?
   4. What is the state of the economy?

C. **Your Competition**
   1. Who are they?
   2. Where are they?
   3. How are you different?

D. **Your Team**
   1. Who will teach with you?
   2. What are their qualifications?
   3. How many teachers will you have?

E. **Business Operation**
   1. How can you best schedule your after-school hours?
   2. What are the possibilities for the future?

F. **Finance**
   1. You must record information in journals and ledgers.
   2. What price must you set so that you can make a profit?
   3. Profit and Loss Statement.
   4. What are the proper circumstances in which to extend or deny credit?
   5. How will you collect overdue accounts?
   6. How much will you pay your teachers?

G. **Advertising/Public Relations**
   How will you use to increase demand and awareness?

H. **Location**
   1. What are the benefits and drawbacks of your location?
   2. Are you in a good family area?
   3. How many parking spaces do you have?

Remember, time well spent now in planning will save you money (and headaches) later.

The Bookkeeping System

Most small businesses can get by with a reasonably uncomplicated record-keeping system. So long as you keep track of what's coming in and going out, along with costs for labor and expenses, you'll be just fine. When money starts pouring in and things get more complicated, then you can hire a bookkeeper.

While you alone are doing the bookkeeping, don't neglect it. It's just a matter of setting aside a couple of hours regularly every week. If you do it while the transactions are still fresh in your mind and the receipts within easy reach, it won't take long.

Forms and Time Savers

Everything should be written down and filed in its proper place. As your business and staff grow, it becomes more and more necessary for all participants to have access to vital information. Organization of the constant inflow of information is the only possible way to keep your business running efficiently.

Pricing

Believe it or not, charging less than your competitor will usually harm you more than help you. How much you charge for your product is important, but the perceived value is even more important. I feel that you should be at the higher end, and you will be perceived as the best.

No matter what your goals are, you will not be able to attain them if you don't make enough money to succeed. To help others, you must stay in business. **Prosper by giving of your talents**.

One of the most common mistakes dance teachers make is to underprice their services. Many people believe that lesser priced services mean lesser quality.

A good example of this is a teacher who was just barely keeping her doors open when she finally hired a business consultant to help diagnose the problem. The consultant's advice was to raise the price of classes. The teacher reacted angrily: "Gee, I can't do that! People won't pay that price!"

"That's right," the consultant replied, "a dance class as cheap as yours can't be that good." The teacher raised the price and more than doubled her enrollment in a few years. To be taken seriously, your price must convey value.

Always Sign Your Own Checks

You're *never* too big or too busy to watch where all the money goes.

Establish a Professional Business

The keys to becoming a professional studio owner can be found at business workshops, seminars, and professional agencies. By this, I don't mean just dance-related organizations or functions. I mean organizations including The National Small Business Association, The Network for Professional Women, or Women Entrepreneurs. I've provided you with the addresses for these and other such groups. Explore as many as you can, and remember, you are a professional.

AWED (American Woman's Economic Development, Inc.)
60 E. 42nd Street, New York, NY 10165
(212)692-9100; (800)222-AWED (outside New York City)
This nonprofit organization offers counseling and training to women who want to launch or expand a business or solve problems. This counseling is available nationwide by phone (AWED pays for the call) or in person (in New York City, Washington, DC, and Los Angeles) for $35 per half-hour session. There's also a toll-free hot line for quick questions – ten-minute sessions for $10. A newsletter, *Woman Entrepreneur*, comes out monthly. Call or write for more information.

SBA (Small Business Association)
For a recorded message on how to start a successful business, dial (800)368-5855. SBA programs include the following:

SCORE (Service Corps of Retired Executives) offers counseling nationwide, assistance with business or marketing plans, and solutions to day-to-day problems.

SBDCs (Small Business Development Centers) are geared to helping start-ups. Each SBDC operates in conjunction with local colleges. The staff includes business-school professors and business professionals, who assist in writing plans, obtaining financing, and conducting market research. (For the location of the SBDC nearest you, contact your SBA District Office.)

WNET (Women's Network for Entrepreneurial Training) recruits successful women business owners to act, for one year, as mentors to women owners of fledgling companies.

Local Chamber of Commerce
Contact your town's chamber of commerce. It is responsible for stimulating business growth in the area.

At the Library
For a list of trade journals or magazines: *Ulrich's International Periodicals Directory* and *Gale Directory of Publications.* For a list of associations: *Encyclopedia of Associations.* For industry directories: *Dun & Bradstreet* or *Standard & Poors.* For articles on retailing and manufacturing: *Business Periodicals Index.* For a list of department stores and their buyers: *Sheldon's Retail Directory.*

For Census Data
Bureau of the Census Customer Services, Washington, DC 20233, (301)763-4100.

Mother's Home Business Network
MHBN, P.O. Box 423, East Meadow, NY 11554
(800)828-2259
This organization offers information and support to mothers who want to work at home. Membership is $25 for 16 months. Some of the entitlements: four issues of the newsletter *Homeworking Mothers;* a booklet *Mothers' Money Making Manual,* with 150 home-business ideas; and two issues of another newsletter, *Kids & Career: New Ideas and Options for Mothers.* Send a self-addressed, stamped envelope for a free brochure.

The National Association for the Cottage Industry
P.O. Box 14850, Chicago, IL 60614
(312)472-8116
For $45 a year, members receive *Cottage Connection*, a newsletter published six times a year. Highlights include good ideas for home-based businesses, along with information on health insurance and on labor and zoning laws. Send a self-addressed, stamped envelope for a free copy of its current newsletter.

Women Entrepreneurs
1275 Market Street, Suite 1300, San Francisco, CA 94103
(415)929-0129

National Association of Women Business Owners
600 South Federal Street, Suite 400, Chicago, IL 60605
(312)246-2330

Association for Small Business Advancement
7507 Standish Place, Rockville, MD 20855
(301)770-6610

National Small Business Association
1155 15th Street NW, 7th Floor, Washington, DC 20005
(202)293-8830

National Women's Forum
1818 N. Street NW, Suite 350, Washington, DC 20036
(202)775-8917

Network for Professional Women
c/o Career Source, 15 Lewis Street, Hartford, CT 06103
(203)247-2011

Network of Women Entrepreneurs
108 East Fremont, Suite 5194, Sunnyvale, CA 94087
(408)720-9520

National Alliance of Professional and Executive Women's Networks – 8600 LaSalle Road, Suite 308, Baltimore, MD 21204
(301)321-6699

National Association for the Self-Employed
2324 Gravel Road, Fort Worth, TX 76118
(817)589-2475

National Association for Women in Careers
7900 Cass Avenue, Suite 115, Darcia, IL 60559
(312)870-8991

National Alliance of Home Based Business Women
P.O. Box 307
Midland Park, NJ 07432

Bank of America
Department 3120
P.O. Box 37000, San Francisco, CA 94137
(415)622-2491
Write the Bank of America for information about its excellent series of publications, *The Small Business Reporter*, including issues on how to start a business, how to finance a business, retail business, and franchising.

Best Employers Association
4201 Birch Street, Newport Beach, CA 92660
(213)756-1000

American Business Women's Association
P.O. Box 8728, 9100 Ward Parkway, Kansas City, MO 64114
(816)361-6621

American Entrepreneurs Association
2311 Pontius Avenue, Los Angeles, CA 90064
(213)478-0437

American Federation of Small Business
407 South Dearborn, Chicago, IL 60605
(312)427-0207

American Society of Professional and Executive Women
1511 Walnut Street, Philadelphia, PA 19102
(215)563-4415

Catalyst
250 Park Avenue South, New York, NY 10003
(212)777-8900
Provides a career information service, a national network of career resource centers, and over 60 publications on careers for women, including entrepreneurship.

Center for Entrepreneurial Management
29 Green Street, New York, NY 10013
(212)925-7304
Through courses and seminars, provides assistance with developing a business plan; obtaining venture capital; organizing an entrepreneurial team; getting patents, trademarks, and copyrights. Maintains an extensive library of information of interest to the entrepreneur.

Center for Family Business
P.O. Box 24268, 5862 Mayfield Road, Cleveland, OH 44124
(216)442-0800
Offers educational programs directed at the family-owned business; topics include small-business management, business succession, and maintaining business continuity.

International Council for Small Business
c/o Donald D. Myers, 304 Harris Hall, University of Missouri
Rolla, MO 65401   (314)341-4568
Working with universities and local school systems, sponsors small-business management seminars throughout the world; members engage in research on issues related to entrepreneurship and the entrepreneur.

National Business League
4324 Georgia Avenue NW, Washington, DC 20001
(202)829-5900
Promotes the economic development of minorities and encourages minority ownership and management of small businesses; has a special committee, Council of Women in Business, that focuses on issues of concern to women.

National Family Business Council
60 Revere Drive, Suite 500, Northbrook, IL 60062
Sponsors seminars on unique problems inherent in running a
family business.

Office of Women's Business Ownership
Small Business Administration (SBA)
1441 L. Street NW, Washington, DC 20416
(202)653-8000
Sponsors University Business Development Centers at colleges
and universities around the country (write them for local addresses); offers many fine publications about start-up, marketing, planning, financing, and general management practices.

SCORE (Service Corps of Retired Executives)
1129 20th Street NW, Suite 410, Washington, DC 20416
(202)653-6279
Organization composed of retired business men and women
that provides actual or potential entrepreneurs with free advice.

The Small Business Foundation of America
20 Park Plaza, Suite 438, Boston, MA 02116
(617)350-5096
Nonprofit organization raises funds for education and research
in small business and sponsors seminars and conferences for
entrepreneurs.

The following three organizations offer special seminars for
entrepreneurs:

The Country Business Brokers
225 Main Street, Brattleboro, VT 05301
(802)254-4504

The School for Entrepreneurs
Tarrytown House, East Sunnyside Land, Tarrytown, NY 10591
(212)933-1232   (914)591-8200

The Entrepreneurship Institute
90 East Wilson Bridge Road, #247, Worthington, OH 43085
(614)855-0585

Clearinghouse on Women's Issues
P.O. Box 70603, Friendship Heights, MD 20813
(301)871-6106
Offers a regular newsletter that details government actions of national or local impact affecting women and minorities – reports on economic and labor issues of .particular interest to entrepreneurs.

Jayne Townsend and Associates
709 Broderick Street, Suite 2, San Francisco, CA 94117
(415)922-3105
Jayne Townsend has compiled a comprehensive directory of women's groups in the western states: $9.00 for one issue, $12 for updated yearly subscription of two issues.

National Council for Research on Women
Sara Delano Roosevelt Memorial House, 47 East 65th Street, New York, NY 10021 (212)570-5001
Conducts and promotes collaborative research on topics of concern to women; acts as clearinghouse for information of interest to women; offers seminars and conferences.

National Women's Mailing List
P.O. Box 68, Jenner, CA 95450 (707)632-5763
Uses computer technology to promote networking between women and women's organizations; maintains databank on women's groups and services.

Small Business Legislative Council
1025 Vermont Avenue NW, Suite 1201, Washington, DC 20006
(202)639-8500
Provides testimony before Congress on issues of concern to entrepreneurs and works on behalf of small-business interests.

The best workshop is the **National Teacher Seminar** workshop held at the Showstopper National Talent Competition Finals. Everyone is welcome at no charge. Call (919)431-8017 for more information.

Finesse Your Way to Success

As much as I hate to admit it, you could read this entire book 100 times and still be missing that little something that makes one studio more successful than another. It's one of those things you just can't put your finger on. It is a *finesse*, a sense of which decisions are the right ones, something you have to figure out for yourself through time and experience.

One example that confronted me had to do with a photo booth. I was convinced it was a sure money-maker. I planned to take the booth to every Showstopper event, and dancers would flock to it to have their picture taken. I had a fancy booth made up for $1,000 and bought a $3,000 camera. Yet, at the first event I took it to, I couldn't find a good place to put it, so I stuck it up on the balcony. Not one person showed the least bit of interest.

You see, no matter how much time and effort I had put into this idea, I had left out one crucial detail. Where was I going to put such a booth? As a result, my sure thing idea was a flop. A studio owner can be 99 percent right, but that 1 percent wrong could be all it takes to damage the business. Be aware of it, be on your toes always, and do your best to look at every angle of every decision you make that affects your studio. Then you can finesse your way to success.

Chapter Twelve
Teacher's Survey

During the Spring of 1991, a survey questionnaire was prepared and distributed to thousands of dance teachers throughout the United States. The following are the results of the responses to those questionnaires.

Chapter Twelve
Teacher's Survey

What do you consider your "drawing area?"

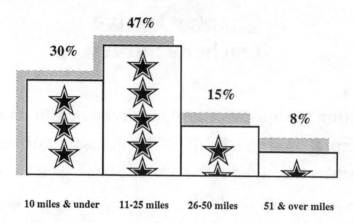

Average: 24 miles

Population of your city.

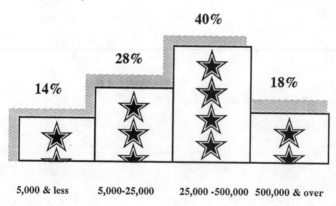

Range: 700 to 4,000,000

Your farthest student travels how far?

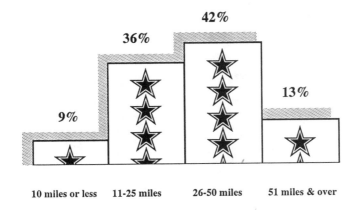

42%

36%

13%

9%

| 10 miles or less | 11-25 miles | 26-50 miles | 51 miles & over |

Range: 5 to 200 miles

Total number of students you have.

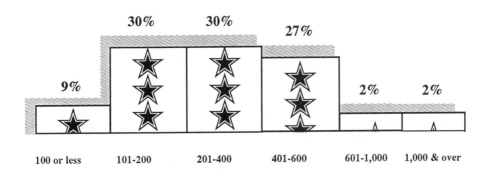

30%   30%

27%

9%

2%   2%

| 100 or less | 101-200 | 201-400 | 401-600 | 601-1,000 | 1,000 & over |

Range: 40 to 2,000

137

How long have you been at your current location?

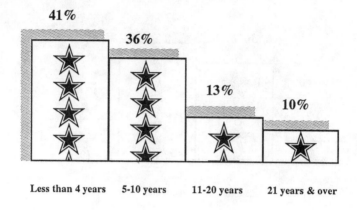

41%

36%

13%

10%

Less than 4 years   5-10 years   11-20 years   21 years & over

Range: 1 month to 36 years

Do you have more than one studio location?

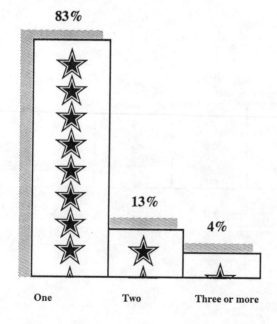

83%

13%

4%

One   Two   Three or more

Total number of teaching classrooms.

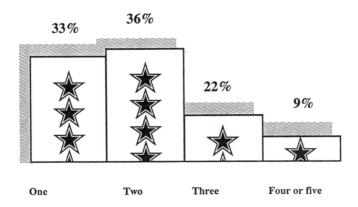

| One | Two | Three | Four or five |

Describe your own dance training (years taken, etc.).

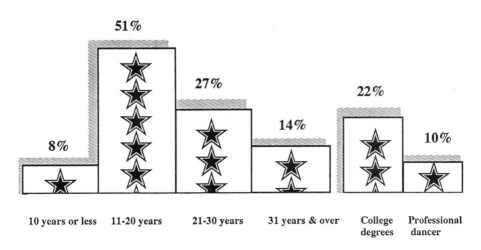

| 10 years or less | 11-20 years | 21-30 years | 31 years & over | College degrees | Professional dancer |

What is your average number of students per dance class?

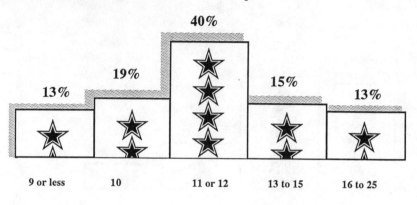

Average: 12

How late do you run classes during the week?

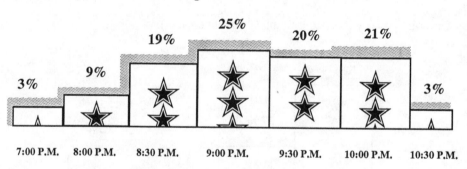

Do you have Saturday classes?

YES 68%

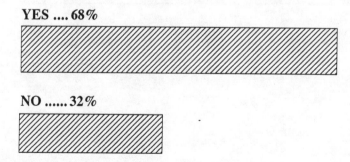

NO 32%

What is your busiest class day?

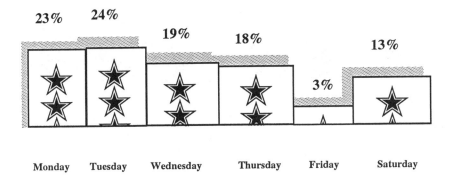

What is your base monthly charge for a one-hour class once a week?

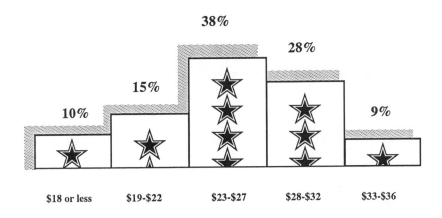

Average: $28.00

Do you give discounts for:

More than one child in a family?

YES 90%

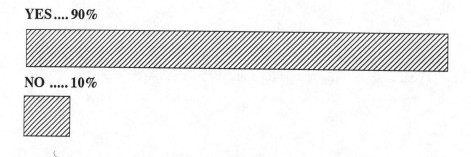

NO 10%

More than one class a week?

YES.... 90%

NO 10%

Do you give any scholarships?

YES ... 57%

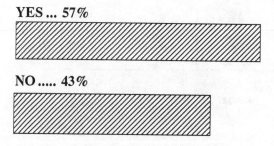

NO 43%

Student teacher's pay.

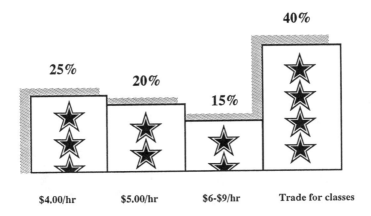

25%   20%   15%   40%

$4.00/hr $5.00/hr $6-$9/hr   Trade for classes

How much do you pay your assistant teacher?

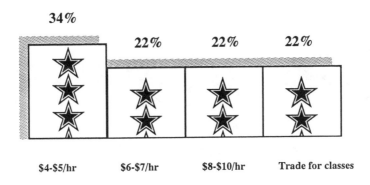

34%   22%   22%   22%

$4-$5/hr $6-$7/hr $8-$10/hr   Trade for classes

How much do you pay a teacher able to conduct his/her own class?

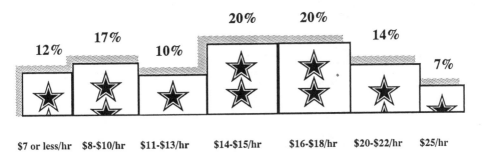

12% 17% 10% 20% 20% 14% 7%

$7 or less/hr $8-$10/hr $11-$13/hr $14-$15/hr $16-$18/hr $20-$22/hr $25/hr

Average: $14.70/hr

143

Do you charge a registration fee? If so, how much?

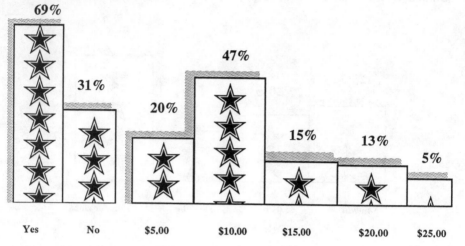

Do you have an annual recital?

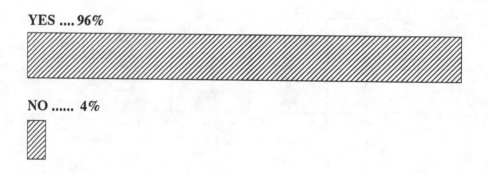

Your average recital costume charge.

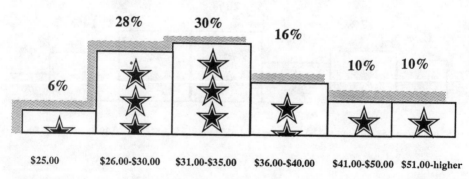

Do you charge a recital fee?

YES 55%

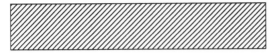

NO 45%

Do you sell recital tickets?

YES 68%

NO 32%

What month is your recital in?

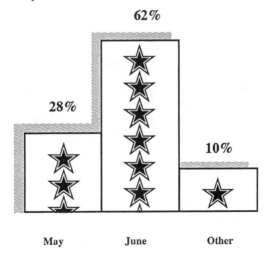

Do you sell ads in your recital program?

YES 33%

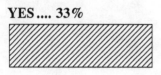

NO 67%

Do you rent or own your own dance studio?

RENT .. 72%

OWN ... 28%

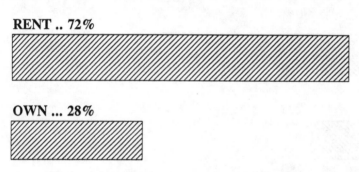

How long has your studio been in business?

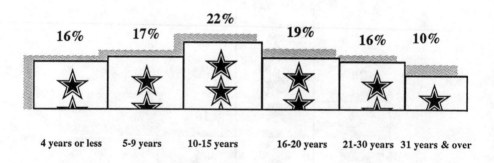

16%   17%   22%   19%   16%   10%

4 years or less   5-9 years   10-15 years   16-20 years   21-30 years   31 years & over

Do you start, inherit, or purchase your dance studio?

START 80%

INHERIT 9%

PURCHASE 11%

Do you teach acrobatics or gymnastics at your studio?

YES 73%

NO 27%

Do you have summer classes?

YES 85%

NO 15%

How long are your summer classes?

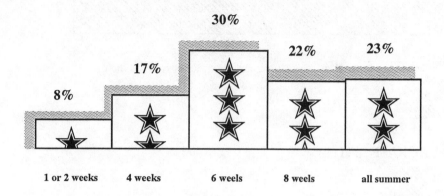

Average number of students per summer class?

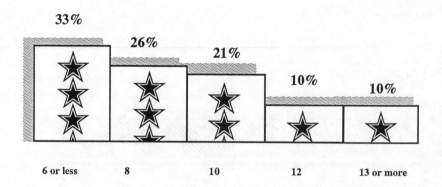

What are some of your best ideas?

Monthly newsletter with important ideas, dates, awards, births of new family members in studio, etc.

Incentive prizes for fund-raiser sales

Report cards for class performance

Trophies for attendance

Open studio free 1-5 P.M. Saturdays with a teacher to help students

Hold auditions for performing groups

Made ballet mandatory for all performing groups and high level students

Studio promotions, such as giving a bike to student who gets most friends to sign up

Keep students busy all year – make dance and arts an important part of their life

Have recital after school is out and charge 1/2 tuition for June

Dancewear shop – require students to wear what I sell; it also helps attract students

Special performing groups

Fund-raising for costumes

Plan a year ahead

Don't allow parents to injure your self-esteem

Regular teachers meetings

Start a ballet company

One free month for students referring someone who enrolls for entire year

Give a t-shirt with registration fee

Mother/daughter number in recital and/or father/daughter number. Now have five adult classes because of it.

Have a dance captain of my competing group

Try to teach as many classes as I can myself

Christmas promotions

Have a flat tuition rate for unlimited classes

Animal mascot for baby numbers

"Bring a friend" discount coupons

Teach 1/2 month in June and collect 1/2 month tuition

Have our recital two nights instead of one (greater show)

Winter showcase with student choreography

Pic-a-Pal week – students bring a friend; if they register, they get a month tuition discount

Do everything in a first-class way

Build own studio instead of rent

Be present in studio to handle public relations

Have a strong staff

Dance companies for all age groups

No videos at recital

If students take jazz, they must take mandatory ballet

Don't have a secretary every week

Have end-of-year pool party with parents performing their child's dance complete with costume and props

No solos in recital

Perform a mini-Nutcracker in December for elderly, sick, and retarded

Give free costumes to beginners

"Moms" class

Do not have a parents committee

Competition fund-raisers

Allow students to take extra classes for free in same subject

Computerized bookkeeping

Having recital in a beautiful, plush auditorium

Start "jazz only" classes for elementary schools

Picture program book – also serves as fund-raiser

Priority on customer service and good attitudes toward costumers

Buy a computer program

Recital fee – that way don't have to hassle with ticket sales

A ballet production for students by audition

Bring a new student who stays for at least three months and get your costume free

Summer dance clinics

Try to mention every child by name in class every week

Speak to parents briefly between classes

Start a parent booster club to raise money

Hire the best teachers I can, and pay them what they are worth

Allow only two parent observation weeks per year

Studio birthday parties

Catchy logo and slogan

Rent a float for parades

Rent a billboard

Have community performances

Go from seven studios to <u>one</u> school

Teach underprivileged children dance one day a week and have my students assist

Separate recital into 1) ages 7 and under 2) ballet 3) tap and jazz

Beautiful reception in lobby after the recital

Wrist-a-Gram – staple note on pre-school wrist so they won't lose important information

What have you found to be your best form of advertising?

Word of mouth	57%
Newspaper	15%
Telephone Yellow Pages	12%
Others:	15%

Local performances	Recital
County fair booth	Brochure
Billboards	Coupons
Signs throughout city	Recital videotape
Press releases	Owner's appearance and attitude

Your goals in this business

Top ten answers:

1. Inspire and turn out quality dancers
2. Financial success
3. Build poise and self-confidence
4. Help students feel good about themselves
5. Develop character, integrity, self-esteem
6. Help students develop love and joy of dance
7. Provide the best dance education possible
8. Prepare students who want to go on to a professional career
9. To have (*number*) of students
10. Open a second studio

Others:

Direct/choreograph nationally

Offer dance to those who can't afford it

Build my own studio

To pass on studio to daughters

Dear Teacher:

Thank you for your creativity, knowledge, and love. *You have made a difference.*

May you peer into your dancers' futures and envision how your studio enriches their lives. Do your best to develop teaching methods that serve each student's needs.

Teach creatively, preparing new and interesting choreography to challenge your students and expand their minds. Through your guidance, they will set higher goals and dream loftier dreams.

Most of all, give your students love and praise and encourage them to pick themselves up and try again if they fail.

If you can do this, you will have ...

The Super Studio!

Resources

All successful people with whom I have had contact are good readers. I strongly suggest the following books as a must:

Keep the Customer, Robert Desatnick. (Jossey-Bass, Inc., 350 Sansome, San Francisco, CA 94104) $8.95

How to Win Friends & Influence People, Dale Carnegie. (Pocket Books, Simon & Schuster, 1230 Avenue of the Americas, New York, NY 10020) $5.95

Doing What You Love, Loving What You Do, Dr. Robert Anthony. (Berkley Publishing, 200 Madison, New York, NY 10016) $7.95

Home Business Handbook. (Putnam Publishing Group, 200 Madison Avenue, New York, NY 10016) $9.95

How to Become Successfully Self-Employed, Brian Smith. (Bob Adams, Inc., 260 Center St., Holbrook, MA 02343) $19.95

Quality is Free, Philip B. Crosby. (Penguin/Viking Books, 375 Hudson, New York, NY 10014) $4.95

Stress for Success, Peter Hanson, M.D. (Ballantine Books, 201 E. 50th St., New York, NY 10022) $4.95

Teach Only Love, Gerald G. Jampolsky. (Bantam Books, Inc., 666 Fifth Avenue, New York, NY 10103) $8.95

What Do You Think of You?, Scott Sheperd, Ph.D. (CompCare, Minneapolis, MN) $6.95

Smart Woman at Work, Terry Ward. (Ballantine Books, 201 E. 50th St., New York, NY 10022) $3.95

You Can Work Your Own Miracles. (Ballantine Books, 201 E. 50th St., New York, NY 10022) $3.95

Making a Difference: 12 Qualities That Make You a Leader, Sheila Murray Bethel. (Berkley Books, 200 Madison Avenue, New York, NY 10016) $7.95

Spirit of Leadership. (Leadership Education and Development, Inc., P.O. Box 3820007, Germantown, TN 38138) $8.95

Can You Cope with Happiness, Joyce Duco. (BNA Corporate Center, Nashville, TN 37217) $4.95

Winning Ways, Gayle Carson. (Berkley Books, 200 Madison Ave., New York, NY 10016) $3.95

Million Dollar Habits, Robert J. Ringer. (Fawcett/Ballantine Books, 201 E. 50th St., New York, NY 10022) $5.95

Winning, David Viscott, M.D. (Pocket Books, Simon & Schuster, 1230 Avenue of Americas, New York, NY 10020) $4.95

The Magic of Thinking Big. (Simon & Schuster, 1230 Avenue of Americas, New York, NY 10020) $7.95

The Success System That Never Fails, W. Clement Stone. (Pocket Books, Simon & Schuster, 1230 Avenue of Americas, New York, NY 10020) $7.95

Being Happy: A Handbook to Greater Confidence and Security, Andrew Matthews. (Price Stern Sloan, 360 N. LaCienega Blvd., Los Angles, CA 90048) $9.95

Winning When It Really Counts, Arch Lustberg. (Pocket Books, Simon & Schuster, 1230 Avenue of Americas, New York, NY 10020) $3.95

Running Through Walls, David Liederman. (Prima Publishing, PO Box 1260LT, Rocklin, CA 95677) $9.95

How to Start, Run, and Stay in Business, Gregory F. Kishel and Patricia Kishel. (John Wiely, 605 Third Ave., New York, NY 10158) $9.95

The Psychology of Winning. (Nightingale-Conant, 7300 N. Lehigh, Chicago, IL 60648) $10.95

The Self-Employed Woman, Jeanette R. Scollard. (Pocket Books, Simon & Schuster, 1230 Avenue of the Americas, New York, NY 10020) $7.95

Be the Boss: Start and Run Your Own Service Business, Sandy Wilson. (Avon Books, 105 Madison Ave., New York, NY 10016) $4.50

Let's Talk Quality, Philip B. Crosby. (Penguin Group, 375 Hudson St., New York, NY 10014) $7.95

Index